THE ART OF CARING

Heart warming stories that illustrate
hope, comfort, and compassion.

TREVOR ROMAIN

Edited by Steven Abrams
Book design by Cory Rivademar

Photograph for *The Light* taken by Randal Alhadeff
All other images, art, and characters created by Trevor Romain

Note from the Author: These stories are based on my memories of the events. Some names and details have been changed for privacy considerations.

ISBN: 978-0-9842722-0-4

Second Edition
10 9 8 7 6 5 4 3 2

©Trevor Romain Foundation, 4412 Spicewood Springs, Suite 705, Austin, TX 78759 • 877-T-Romain • www.TrevorRomainFoundation.org

For everyone who is dedicated to making the world a better place for others.

Foreword

Trevor Romain has the rare ability to connect quickly and communicate effectively with children and young adults. This book is a reflection and expression of that gift.

I am thrilled the USO (United Service Organizations) has partnered with Trevor since 2007 when he began touring with us and taking his message to military children on how to deal with such difficult issues as divorce, homework and bullies. As our partnership has progressed, Trevor expanded his caring message and created a Memory Kit to help the children of those troops who have fallen during their service to our country cope with the loss and to understand it is okay to feel sad and to miss their mom or dad.

Trevor and I met at a brainstorming meeting to explore other ways we could support military children. What an incredible meeting—Trevor is totally committed to helping kids and is a natural extension of the USO's mission to "lift the spirits of troops and their families." We decided to tackle two tough topics for military kids—deployments and the visible as well as invisible wounds of war. As a result, the USO expanded our partnership with Trevor by creating two DVD's to cover these critically important topics. The first DVD, *With You All the Way*, helps children deal with their feelings about their parent deploying away from home. The second DVD, *Camp Hero*, helps kids deal with their feelings about the changes their parent often has when they come home after deployment. In this DVD, Trevor helps kids understand that their parents may be dealing with both visible and invisible wounds and that their parents need their love and support. It also helps them understand their parent wants to be there for them and that everything will be okay over time.

In this second edition of *The Art of Caring*, Trevor shares his positive and uplifting expressions of hope and comfort that will remain with kids as they mature. One amazing aspect of this book is there is something in it for everyone: kids, young adults, parents, professional counselors, and hospice workers. Trevor's main message to everyone he meets is to listen to your kids—listen instead of telling them what you think they want to hear. Kids want to be heard and understood. In *The Art of Caring*, Trevor's passion for this cause shines through.

I welcome you to open your heart and mind to the important message Trevor brings to children the world over. The USO is very proud of our partnership with Trevor Romain and shares his deep and lasting commitment to help our military families.

Sloan Gibson
President of the USO

Table of Contents

Preface

On a recent trip home to South Africa, I had the privilege of meeting Nelson Mandela at his house in Houghton, Johannesburg. I was sitting across from the man who engineered the dismantling of apartheid in South Africa, who was jailed for twenty-seven years for standing up for justice, and whose steadfastness and incredible belief in what was right for the people in the region changed history. I was sitting with one of my roes. It was a humbling experience.

During our short visit, over a cup of tea, Mr. Mandela and I spoke about the plight of suffering children. He told me that teaching children compassion is something the world must strive to do. I shared with him some of the experiences I'd had with children during my travels to the Congo, Burundi, and Uganda, and my work with terminally ill children.

I found Nelson Mandela to be a quiet, wise, and compassionate man. He exuded an energy that seemed to envelop my body and touch my soul. He did not speak for the sake of speaking, but when he did talk, his voice was soothing, steady, and quietly comforting.

He listened intently, without uttering a word while I poured my heart out, then he put his old, unsteady hand on mine and made me promise to retell my stories to anyone who would listen. "Keep these stories alive," Mr. Mandela said, smiling. "They are an important way for people to share and learn from each other's experiences. When a person dies, their library of stories dies with them."

By compiling this book, I am keeping my promise to the honorable Mr. Mandela, fondly known as Madiba, the grandfather of South Africa, to keep my stories alive.

The Art of Caring

1. **The Reason**

Everyone's life is a string of moments. Some moments are big, some are small, some we remember and some we don't. And sometimes an amazing moment will impact our lives in the most profound of ways. For me, I can point to one particular breakthrough moment that changed my life forever—a brilliant moment that lives in my mind like a lone sparkler sending out shimmering rays on a pitch-black night. A moment that was born when I was a young soldier in the army but quickly pushed aside because I was too young and way too inexperienced to know how to deal with it.

Instead, I pursued a career in advertising. I rose in the

ranks to become a creative director at an advertising agency. It was a prestigious, highly lucrative job. And I was good at it. I had dozens of awards to prove it. I thought my life was set.

There was nothing particularly unique about the day everything changed. I had pulled an all-nighter creating an advertising campaign for a new client. The campaign was a good one. I felt great about it and was confident that the client would love the ideas I was presenting. Just another day at the office.

But the client reviewed the campaign with a look of disdain. "Nah," he said, chomping on a cigar. "This is bad. I hate it." He wanted me to make the logo fill the entire page. He wanted the art I worked on all night gone.

And then it hit me. The ad had no heart. No soul. Just like all the work I'd been doing. And I got really angry. Not at the client, but at myself. Because just then I remembered a promise I had made twenty years before. A promise I had not kept.

It happened when I was in the army in South Africa. I was walking through a field hospital filled with kids from small rural villages who had been brought to the clinic for treatment from the army medical corps. The conditions were abysmal. There were almost six kids per bed, it was nauseatingly hot, and there were flies everywhere, especially around the corners of the children's eyes and mouths.

As I was walked down the center aisle, I caught sight of a little boy who was about five years old sitting on the edge of one of the hospital beds. We locked eyes, his huge, brown eyes pleading. I noticed with shock that he had no legs. Instead I saw dirty bandages wrapped around two stumps. The boy had lost his legs in a landmine accident on the Angolan border.

As I walked by, the little boy put up his hands and said "Sir, can you please hold me?"

I will never forget the haunting look of sadness in his eyes. Huge tears rolled slowly down his cheeks and dropped to the floor, their significance lost in the dust and grime of war.

The Sergeant Major, who was walking alongside me, grabbed my arm and pulled me away from the child.

"Romain," he grunted. "Leave him alone." We were there for security. We weren't to get emotionally involved.

As the Sergeant Major pulled me away, the little boy spoke again. His broken, choked-up whisper tugged at me from behind.

"Sir, please, please can you just hold me?"

Something happened to me that moment that I will never forget. It felt like a hand came out of the sky, reached inside me, and flipped a switch that turned on my soul.

I pushed the Sergeant Major's hand away, walked back and picked up the little boy. His strength surprised me. I have never been held so tightly in my life. Trembling through his anguish, the little boy clung to me for all he was worth.

He put his head against my chest and he began to cry. His tears ran down inside my shirt and touched my heart. I held that little boy with my arms, my heart, and my soul. With every ounce of compassion in my being, I held him. I never wanted to let him go, ever.

With that little boy in my arms I made myself a promise. A

promise that I would never waste a second of my valuable life. That I would use my creative talents to change the world for children.

But I didn't.

I finished my stint in the army and went into advertising because it was safe and the money was good and everyone told me that it was impossible to make a living writing and illustrating children's books. And I believed them. I was so wrapped up in the glamour of advertising that I stopped listening to myself and totally ignored my inner voice. I got sucked into the advertising vortex. I allowed client after client to put my work down, destroy my exciting ideas, and turn me into a cynic who spent every day using my talents to convince consumers to buy things they didn't need.

Then one day I promptly resigned. The cigar-chomping client wasn't the reason I quit that day, but for some reason he triggered the little boy's voice and the promise I had made to myself in the army.

My wife and I discussed the situation and both decided that I *had* to follow my dream.

I woke up the next day, sat in front of my yellow pad and started my new job as an unpublished children's author and illustrator.

Although getting started was difficult and sometimes frustrating, the sheer passion and joy of doing what I love was there. And it still is. I have been hungry, rejected, underappreciated and often ignored, but I love what I do. I have been writing full time for fifteen years now and I am one of the happiest people I have ever met.

During my journey, after every book rejection I received, I heard the little boy's voice in my head saying, "Sir, please can you just hold me?" And in my heart and soul I did.

And I still do. Based on my life's mission, which was sparked by the little boy in the field hospital, I have taken the content of my books and stories and—with my business partners Woody and Ronda Englander—have used the material to create animated videos, self-help books for kids, picture books, educational curricula, music and a PBS television series. We have also created a nonprofit foundation to help kids facing adversity, kids just like that little boy who inspired me.

People often ask me why I have dedicated my life to working with children, why I subject myself to the heartbreaking stories and gut-wrenching events surrounding many of the kids I have chosen to work with. My answer is always the same: I do what I do because a little voice reminded me that there is a shortage of caring and compassion in the world and that the smallest things can make the biggest difference.

And I'm not done yet. I still hear the little boy's voice.

2. Max

  As a volunteer at children's hospitals, I've had memories that I will always treasure, and I have made many amazing friendships. One such friend was a young boy named Max, who was fighting bone cancer. Max was a mischievous, sweet kid with a great sense of humor, so it wasn't a total surprise when he turned to me on one of my visits and asked, "What's going to happen when I die?"

  I was about to answer him when his mother jumped off the chair and rushed over to the bed. "You are not going to die," she said, trying to keep his spirits up.

  "Okay," replied Max.

  After working with sick children for as long as I have, I feel comfortable talking with them about things that no one else wants to speak about. So, when his mother left the room I turned to Max. "We're all going to die one day," I said. "I'm going to die, my mom's going to die, and you're going to die."

"I know that," said Max with his usual matter of fact attitude. "I'm not stupid."

"Then what do you mean?" I asked.

"I want to know what's going to happen when I die," he said, calmly.

"Well, I believe people go to heaven," I said. "Different religions believe different things, but I believe we go to heaven."

"Yeah, me too," said Max, thoughtfully.

"You know, talking about heaven makes me think of my grandfather," I said. "Well, I'll tell you what. If you die from this disease and you're still a kid, when you get to heaven, ask for my grandfather; his name is Ted. He lives there."

Max looked at me suspiciously. Because I was always joking and teasing Max, and telling him crazy stories, he started calling me the *Doctor of Mischief,* so his skepticism was well earned.

"My grandfather died many years ago," I said. "But he was the most amazing guy. Everybody loved him and he was one of those grandfathers you just want to hug. I'm sure he's up there doing wonderful things, especially helping kids. Kids loved him."

Max folded his arms and frowned at me.

"Just ask for him when you get there," I said. "He'll get you checked in and I'm sure he'll get you a good room. He knows a lot of people."

"Do you know how many people are in heaven?" Max yelled. "I'll never find him!"

"Relax, it's okay," I said. I tore a piece of paper out of my journal and drew a picture of my grandfather. I gave him the picture and watched a smile spread across his face.

"That's my grandfather Ted," I said, pointing to the picture.

"Thanks," said Max. Max took the picture of my grandfather and stuck it on the corkboard above his bed where all his get-well cards were pinned. From then on, whenever I went into his hospital room as the *Doctor of Mischief,* and teased him, Max threatened to tell my grandfather when he saw him. It got to the point where he would just point to that picture of my grandfather whenever I walked into his room.

I'm very sad to say Max died six months later. His parents asked me to deliver the eulogy at his funeral. I was honored to do so and planned a stand-up comedy–style memorial celebrating Max's life, instead of a eulogy mourning his death. On the day of his funeral, I was taken aback when I got to the church and realized it was an open casket ceremony. I skirted around the coffin and went into the sanctuary. I did not want to see Max lying in his casket. I wanted to remember him pointing at the picture of my grandfather with his mischievous face.

The open coffin was wheeled in and placed alongside the pulpit. The priest delivered the sermon and asked me to deliver the eulogy. I went up to the pulpit and eulogized my friend Max, all the time trying not to look at him lying in the coffin alongside where I was standing. I told the congregation about some of the crazy things Max had done during his battle with cancer, like putting a snake in the bedside table and scaring a nurse half to death.

I told them about the time Max borrowed an idea from an Erma Bombeck book and put apple juice in his urine sample container. When the nurse came to collect the sample he said, "Look it's all milky," and he held up the bottle for the nurse to see.

"Sure is," she said, squinting at the container.

"Well I'd better pass it through again," he said, quickly opening the container and taking a sip. The nurse screamed and Max almost choked with laughter. As I completed this story the congregation burst into uncontrollable giggles.

"Yup," I said. "Max was one in a million. He changed the way I look at life and he changed the way I look at death." Talking about Max and missing him, I braved a glance at the coffin. I saw Max lying comfortably amongst a pile of satin pillows. He was dressed in a black tuxedo with a red bow tie. He looked so peaceful. He was lying with his hands resting on his chest and around him in his coffin were all his childhood toys.

His dad had polished up his baseball mitt, which lay on his stomach cradling a brand new baseball. His collection of teddy bears sat along the edge of the coffin looking at him sadly. His mom had ironed his softball outfit and it lay in the coffin clean and pressed. I am so glad I glanced over at Max because he looked so calm and comfortable. He did not appear sad or in pain. Then suddenly I froze. Because Max, surrounded by the special keepsakes from his life, was holding the picture of my grandfather. Seeing the picture of my grandfather with Max like that, I understood the power of hope and the value of listening. In that extraordinary moment, I recognized the difference each and every one of us can make in someone's life, often without even realizing it.

3. Drawing Hope

The Republic of Burundi is one of the poorest countries in the world. It is still suffering from the aftereffects of a twelve-year ethnic civil war that claimed hundreds of thousands of lives. While democracy was restored in 2005, the country is unstable and warlords still hold court in some areas. And in a country of subsistence farmers, floods and droughts over the years have only compounded the problem, pushing over half the population below the poverty line.

As one might imagine, in these incredibly tough conditions children suffer terribly. I was invited to accompany Ms. Radhika Coomaraswamy, the United Nations Under-Secretary-General, Special Representative for Children and Armed Conflict, to work with a group of children at an orphanage in Bujumbura, the nation's capital. I was obviously worried about the dangers of traveling to Burundi, but being embedded in the United Nations contingency made the trip a lot safer.

All of my uncertainties disappeared once I started working with the wonderful kids in the orphanage. We were in a makeshift classroom with dirt-covered floors and no glass in the windows. The room was dark, close, and depressing in the equatorial heat. At first, the children gazed blankly at me, constantly swatting the flies away from their eyes and expressionless faces. These kids had been through hell—many of the orphaned boys and girls had been raped, abused, prostituted, and then abandoned.

As we were about to start, I noticed that a young boy dressed in a traditional Burundian drumming outfit was watching me through one of the windows. He was draped in red, green, and white toga-like sheets tied in a knot on the shoulder. Round his neck he wore a string of white beads. I invited him to join us but he just stood there, leaning on a walking stick, watching. I could see the sadness in his eyes and it tugged at me. I invited him in again, but he didn't budge. He just stood outside the window and stared.

I respected his decision and turned back to the classroom. My aim was to help the kids express their worries and feelings by drawing pictures of their pain and then having them follow up with drawings of their hopes and wishes. I took a blank piece of paper and did a drawing depicting the pain I felt when my father passed away. It was a dark picture with lots of clouds swirling in a squiggle of angry lines. As I drew I pressed hard on the paper, telling the kids in the class how the heavy, rough lines represented the anger of losing my father. Among the swirls I drew a person curled up in a ball and told them that was me in the picture, experiencing the pain of my father's death. As hard as I tried I could not stop myself from getting misty-eyed when I held up the picture for the kids to see.

Exposing my own pain stirred something within these kids. One little girl wiped away her own tears as I shared my grief. It was incredible. I could feel invisible hugs reaching out from every one of the kids in the room, from children who have experienced more horror and hardships than I'll ever know. The kids looked around at each other and began nodding and discussing my picture as they whispered amongst themselves.

I put the painful picture aside and drew a picture of my hopes and dreams for the future. I drew a happy picture with a boy standing on top of a hill with his arms reaching up to a star. I used as many warm colors as I could. The kids connected with the picture and began to chatter excitedly. I still remember the smiles on the kids' faces as they discussed my picture and suggested more things for me to include on the page, like flowers, the sun, and even kids eating ice cream.

I invited the kids to repeat what I had done, to draw a picture of their own pain, look at the drawing, and acknowledge the emotions evoked by the picture—and then to draw their future hopes and dreams. The mood in the entire room shifted. I could feel the children's emotions change as they drew. It's amazing how cathartic simple lines on a piece of paper can be—how taking pain and suffering from your heart and putting it on paper can make the pain and hurt easier to process and clearer to see.

As they drew, I saw the children grow and bloom. It was like a time-lapse film of a flower opening. And just like a blossoming bud, the children seemed to unfold from tight, curled-up balls void of color or vibrancy, and open into magnificent flowers. When we were done drawing, the kids danced around me and proudly showed off their pictures. At the end of the session, the kids surrounded me in a group hug that I can still feel to this day.

As the children left, I stayed behind to gather my things and to talk to the social worker for the orphanage. I felt like I'd really connected with the kids. But as I was about to leave, a movement at the door caught my eye. It was the young boy in the traditional Burundian drumming outfit who watched me through the window at the beginning of the session. He was now standing in the doorway. In his hand he held a blank piece of drawing paper. In his eyes he held that now familiar vacant stare. He lifted the paper slowly toward me.

"Okay buddy," I said, patting him on the back. "Have a seat. Let's see if we can draw us a little hope and happiness, shall we?"

And we did.

4. The Sunflower

At only twelve years old, Nicole had more vision and hope than her entire family and all of her doctors and nurses put together. She loved horses, and always talked about wanting to ride on a white horse on top of the clouds in a blue, blue sky. She dreamed of being free from the tubes that bound her to her bed.

When I met Nicole, she was undergoing chemotherapy at the Johannesburg General Hospital. Her condition gave her every excuse in the world not to go to school, but she really wanted to learn. As a favor to the family, her teacher came to the hospital a few times a week and shared with Nicole what the other kids had been learning in her absence.

One day I was at the hospital and the teacher was explaining how sunflower seeds sprout when they are placed in a moist cotton ball. The teacher gave Nicole seeds and a cotton ball of her own, and she was thrilled when after a few days the seeds actually started sprouting. "Mom," she said excitedly, holding up a tiny sprout, "please bring me a little planter with some sand when you come tomorrow." Nicole wanted to plant the sprout and watch it grow into a giant sunflower.

Her mother frowned at the windowless intensive care unit. "It might be too dark in here," she said. A nurse who was adjusting Nicole's IV medication nodded in agreement.

"I'll put it under this light," Nicole persisted, pointing to her bedside lamp.

Her mother patted her on the arm gently. "It's okay, sweetie. You can plant a whole field of sunflowers when you go home."

"What if I never go home?" said Nicole.

"C'mon honey," said her mom, "of course you're going to go home."

"I just love sunflowers," said Nicole, "I really do. They make me so happy. I bet heaven is full of sunflowers."

"You've got to stay positive." said Nicole's mother. I looked at Nicole as her mother turned to pin a greeting card on the board alongside the bed. Nicole shrugged. I winked at her. She winked back at me and smiled. The next day Nicole's mother brought a planter filled with dirt and Nicole planted her little sprout with trembling hands.

A few days later I was driving along the road when I noticed a patch of giant sunflowers in a garden. I pulled over. These beautiful golden flowers were as tall as I and seemed to reach for the sun. I don't know what got into me but I jumped the fence and picked one of the magnificent flowers. A very agitated Doberman sent me scrambling back over the fence in a hurry.

I couldn't wait to tell Nicole the story. I knew she was going to crack up at my expense. I put the sunflower in an old wine bottle and drove to the hospital. When I got there I was told by the staff that only family were allowed to see Nicole. They said she had taken a turn for the worse and was "unconscious but comfortable."

My friend Pat was a nurse at the hospital. I asked her to take the flower and put it next to Nicole's bed so she could see what her little sprout was going to look like when it grew up. Nicole did not regain consciousness for almost a week. Pat told me the first thing Nicole saw when she woke up was the sunflower on the bedside table.

"See," she said. "I knew it would grow! People just need to get a little faith around here." After that, Pat says Nicole yawned, stretched and said, "I just love sunflowers. I really do. They make me so happy." She smiled and closed her eyes. She never opened them again.

5. The Golden Moment

There is a place in Botswana, Southern Africa, called the Okavango Delta. Called the Jewel of Africa, it is the largest inland delta in the world. Fed from the rains in Angola, the flood waters make their way to the Kalahari Desert, creating a massive maze of lagoons, channels, and small lush islands. Thousands of plants bloom and thrive during the floods. Forests lining the banks of the waters offer shelter to the parade of animals who are drawn to the rising waters. Large herds of antelope and wildebeest mingle with elephants and giraffes, followed closely by lions, hyenas, and other predators. The place is absolutely breathtaking—the most beautiful place I have ever seen.

It was there, floating on the calm delta waters and surrounded by exotic wildlife and lush plants, that for the first time in my life I felt a true connection to the universe. I was sitting in a dugout canoe called a *mokoro*, with a guide named Vusi. I sat up front while Vusi stood in the back, using a long oar to push the canoe quietly along the sacred delta.

We passed hippos, giraffes, and hundreds of zebras foraging in the bush. The primal beauty of the landscape was humbling. It reminded me that I'm not as important as I sometimes think I am. Facing nature on such a grand scale, the countless trees and plants, the predators and prey, the wide expanse, and the unending sky can all make you feel that your very existence is a mere blink in time.

It was late afternoon and Vusi positioned the dugout so that we could view the sunset from a good vantage point. "They call this the golden moment," he said, pointing to the setting sun, which now bathed the entire delta in a rich golden wash.

"I can see why," I replied.

"It's not because of the color," he said, smiling. Confused, I asked what he meant. "Wait," he replied. The sun, a golden ball, slowly rolled over the horizon. "Listen," he said, bowing his head and closing his eyes. I heard nothing but the loud cacophony of day insects simultaneously trying to have their final say before nightfall. I was really amazed at how loud they were. Then the sun was gone.

Suddenly, all at once the sounds of the day insects stopped completely. Silence drifted across the delta in an indescribable wave. Nothing stirred. Complete stillness. Even the water seemed to stop lapping against the side of the canoe. At that moment the world seemed to take a deep breath. I heard it. I felt it. I became part of it. A total calm that only lasted a few seconds, but it felt like an eternity.

Then, almost as one, the clamor of the night insects suddenly filled the empty void. The noise was so loud I could hardly hear Vusi speak. "That was the golden moment," he said, smiling coyly. "Did you hear the breath?" he asked. "That time between the day and night insects?" I nodded. "That was God's breath," he said.

Vusi turned the boat and moved us across the delta. As we slid silently toward the rising moon, I realized that our very existence is made up of a million magnificent moments strung together on a delicate thread we call life. I understood the value of individual moments that day—not the importance of days or weeks or months or years, but single moments...valuable seconds that are constantly passing us by.

6. The Blossom

I have spent many years visiting schools in the United States and in other countries around the world, and I have spoken to hundreds of thousands of children during those visits. Memories of most of those talks have faded into the past, but every now and then, something happens during a visit that makes the moment unforgettable.

One visit in particular stands out. I was speaking to a class of second graders in Newport Beach, California about making a difference in other people's lives. I dared the kids in the class to stand up for those who are being put down and include those who are being left out.

"Have any of you been left out or put down?" I asked. Nobody responded. I found out later it was because there was a bully in the class, and he was watching the other kids intently as they contemplated whether to answer or not.

I looked around the class and noticed a little girl in the corner shy away. It seemed like she wanted to raise her hand, that she wanted to say something, but was afraid to do so. Finally, the little girl, whose name was Ruth, slowly and ever so slightly raised the fingers of her hand. She was sitting on the edge of the class and was all but hidden in a large sweater. All I could see of Ruth was the little round glasses on her nose and the anxious look in her eyes.

"It's okay if you don't feel comfortable telling us, but have you ever been bullied?" I asked her, gently. I could feel the class tense up. She nodded, sheepishly. "How did it feel?" I asked.

"It was bad," she replied. "Sometimes I don't want to come to school." I smiled and nodded my encouragement to Ruth, but she looked down at her desk and sighed. "One time I wished I was dead," she said. The room went quiet. The other kids shifted in the seats. I noticed the teacher turn away, crying.

With downcast eyes, Ruth seemed to withdraw deeper into her sweater. I calmly walked up to her desk. "Thank you for having the guts to say that," I said. "You are a real brave person for speaking up. For that I need to give you a big hug." I leaned over and hugged her. I could not believe how tiny she was. "You don't deserve to be treated like that," I said. "You are one cool kid."

I went back to the front of the class and continued talking. As I spoke and asked the class questions, I noticed Ruth emerging from her sweater like a flower growing out of the ground. She began to sit up, and later she even raised her hand when I asked questions. It was heartwarming to see her little face fill with color as she blossomed right in front of me. After the class was over, the teacher told me that Ruth hardly ever asked questions, mostly hiding in that sweater of hers.

A week later I received an e-mail from Ruth that made me cry. "Dear Mr. Trevor," she wrote. "Thank you for making me famous at my school. Everyone wants to be my friend."

My experience in that classroom was yet another reminder to me of how the smallest things can make the biggest difference. I continue to learn that one doesn't have to be Mother Teresa or Nelson Mandela to make a great impact on someone else's life. Sometimes it's just a matter of lending an ear to those in need, and simply being there to support them. Ordinary people like you and me have the ability to change the world, one small act of compassion at a time...sometimes without even realizing it.

7. The Wishing Ceremony

The Botshabelo community is situated on 99 acres of farmland in the Magaliesberg mountains, about a two-hour drive from Johannesburg in South Africa. I've visited Botshabelo a number of times. Founded by my dear friends Con and Marion Cloete, Botshabelo is an incredible self-sustaining farm and eco-village for orphans from HIV/AIDS, strife, and poverty.

On one of my trips there I was invited to join Marion, her three daughters, and about thirty kids of all ages for what they call a Wishing Ceremony. We walked single file through the bush and up a winding path to the top of a small hill. Some of the kids held hands and some simply walked alone, sweetly comfortable with themselves. On the top of the hill sat a gnarled old thorn tree with a pile of stones under it. We sat beneath the tree, in a circle, around the stones.

The ceremony was beautiful and incredibly powerful. The group of normally active and excited children sat respectfully, waiting for Marion to speak. Once everyone was settled, she asked all of the children to pick up a stone and place it on the pile while making a wish for themselves and anyone else they would like to wish for. Most of the children in the group had lost one or both of their parents to AIDS. Some of the children had HIV/AIDS themselves. Many in the group—some as young as four or five—had been raped or prostituted, an epidemic in South Africa, where a child is raped every four minutes. In the safety of Marion's wishing circle, child after child spoke of their wishes and hopes.

One tiny girl hoped that her mother was not crying anymore, now that she was in heaven. One little boy said he hoped the man who raped him was not hurting other children. As he spoke a big tear ran down his cheek and dropped into the pile of wishing stones. When he sat down, Marion reached out and pulled his little body toward her, holding him tightly as she kissed the tears on his cheeks. Another boy who was about six thanked Marion for taking care of all the kids in the village.

Hopalang, a four-year-old who I had met on a previous visit, didn't say anything, but as he placed his stone on the pile he smiled, as if wishing the love, support, and nurturing that filled his potbellied little body would never stop. Maki, a beautiful girl who was fifteen or sixteen, cried desperately for her mother and father who both died of AIDS and left her with nothing but painful, terrifying, gut-wrenching memories. Marion wished that the children in the group who were in terrible emotional pain would soon find the smiles that had been stolen from them. My wish was that the children continue getting the comfort and support they so desperately need from the orphanage.

To end the ceremony, Marion made a last wish for all the children in the world who were being raped, hurt, or orphaned at that very moment. When she finished speaking, the children all reached over and silently placed a final rock on the pile. As that happened, I felt this incredible sense of well-being envelop my entire body. I think it's the closest I have come to what one might call a religious experience. I can honestly say that at that moment, I truly felt the presence of the guardian angels who were standing behind each and every child in the group. I think I heard the gentle rustle of their wings as we stood in silence, although it could have been God's sigh moving the tall savanna grass around us. We all stood in silence around the pile of rocks with our arms around each other, as our wishes rose from the huddled group and swirled toward the heavens in a wonderful plume of hope.

Nobody spoke as we made our way back down the path to the village. I hung back as we passed the village cemetery and stopped off at a grave that was marked by an infant's bottle and a stuffed animal. There is not enough money at Botshabelo to have gravestones, and because of this, most of the children's graves are marked by the children's own meager belongings.

The grave I stopped at belongs to Demi, a little girl I met on my last visit to the orphanage. She was twelve days old when I met her. Her mother had died during childbirth and Demi was born prematurely. Demi and I bonded instantly, and I held this tiny little twelve-day-old baby the entire day. She died during her sixth month, due to complications from premature birth and awful medical ineptness. I kneeled down at the grave and spoke to Demi. Suddenly, thoughts of her and the emotions stirred up from the Wishing Ceremony opened the floodgates. I began to sob.

A hand suddenly touched me on the shoulder. It was Hopalang, the four-year-old. Ever the inquisitive little investigator he had wandered over from the group to see what I was doing. "It's okay to cry," he said, patting me on the shoulder as I crouched alongside the grave. He wiped my cheek with his pudgy little hand. Then he patted me gently on the head. I looked up at this amazing child and smiled. With a bursting heart, I hoisted Hopalang onto my back and carried this true angel down the hill and into the village.

8. Reading on the Roof

Megan Stento was a beautiful child, with a smile that could reach across an entire room and hug you unconditionally. She was funny and feisty, and the effects of chemotherapy and grueling radiation sessions did not dampen her wonderful demeanor. She stood at the door of death with a baseball bat and said *Come and get me.*

Visiting Megan one morning, I told her about a new book I had just written. "I'm going to dedicate the book to you," I said. "It's called *The Other Side Of The Invisible Fence.*" Megan thanked me softly. Her illness had left her pale and thin. The treatment had taken her hair. She looked even smaller in the large hospital bed. "As soon as the book comes out, I'll read it to you," I offered.

Megan said nothing for a few seconds. She looked at me with a glimmer in her eye. "You'll have to read real loud if I'm in heaven."

"I will," I said. "If you die before this book comes out I'll climb on the roof of my house and read so darn loud you'll hear me all the way up there." Megan fought an incredible battle, but she was no match for the savage cancer. She died only days after our conversation.

I spoke to Megan's mom, Becky, after the funeral. She asked me if I was going to keep my promise to Megan. I thought about sitting on my roof reading to the sky, to Megan. "Of course," I said, fighting back my tears.

Becky called me later that day and asked if the family could come over to my house when I climbed on the roof to read the book. She thought it would be a good memorial to Megan. "Absolutely," I told her.

Becky called me the next day and asked if I wouldn't mind very much if Megan's class came to the reading on the roof. "I would love that," I told her.

A few days later, the principal of Megan's school called and asked if the entire school could come to the reading on the roof. That's when I said, "I don't think it's possible. My garden is too small."

Showing the same determination and feisty spirit as her daughter, by the next morning, Becky had arranged for me to do the reading on the roof of the Laguna Gloria Art Museum here in Austin, Texas. The location was ideal. The two-story building had a flat roof and was surrounded by a beautifully manicured green lawn.

It rained the entire week before the reading, but on the morning of the event, as I climbed the stairs to the roof, the sun came out and bathed the entire garden in a warm golden light. After climbing the stairs, I approached the small wall running around the perimeter of the roof, and looked over the edge. My heart stopped. Spread across the lawn, sitting on chairs and blankets, were almost a thousand people.

The entire crowd was completely silent. No words were spoken but I could feel their collective hearts singing together like a giant silent choir. The only sound I heard was the chirping of happy birds in the woods surrounding the lawn and the occasional barking of a dog way off in the distance.

I looked up into the sky and read the book to Megan.

9. The Catch

When I was eight years old my father took me fishing. We drove eight or nine miles from my grandfather's farm to the Vaal River which separated the Transvaal and the Orange Free State provinces in central South Africa. It was spring and the leaves on the trees were a million shades of fresh green. The fishing spot was a small clearing between the tall blue gum trees on the riverbank. We put out a huge blanket my mother had given us, and I snooped around the immediate area while my father set up.

When I got back from my exploring, I found everything ready. Two folding chairs were set up facing the lake. Two fishing poles were loaded and ready to go. My father cast my line for me and rested the fishing pole on a Y-shaped twig he'd cut from one of the trees. "Now don't take your eye off that pole," he said.

"The minute it moves, you grab it and jerk it like I showed you."
He threw in his own line and rested it on another Y-shaped
stick. Then he opened the newspaper and settled back into his
chair.

Within thirteen seconds I was bored. I drew patterns on
the sand around the chair with my shoes. Then I leaned far back
on my chair and tried to see if I could see any stars in the deep
blue sky. I knew the stars were there somewhere. Suddenly I
lost my balance and fell over backwards. I hit the beach hard
and winded myself.

I looked at my dad, hoping he'd rush over and comfort me.
He lowered his newspaper slowly. "You've got to be very quiet
when you're fishing," he said. Before he could lift the newspaper
again, my line jerked so hard that it pulled the pole off the stick
and almost into the water. My father jumped up and caught the
line. My father grabbed me by the collar and pulled me over
toward him. "Here, reel it in!" he said, excitedly. "It's your first
fish!"

I was scared and elated. I grabbed the pole and clumsily
reeled in the line. The line got tighter and tighter until it was
almost impossible to reel anymore. Then I jerked the pole back
and suddenly the line gave. I thought I'd lost the fish, but I'd
actually pulled it right out of the water. It landed at my feet
flipping and jumping as it gasped for air. I was horrified.

"All right," yelled my father excitedly. "Now put your foot on
it and let's get rid of the hook."

The fish looked at me. I knew it was scared. I raised my foot
and placed it gently on the fish's body. The fish jerked away then

suddenly jumped toward me. I screamed and ran. My father grabbed the fish and brought it over to me. It was squirming in his hand, mouth gaping. The hook had ripped through the inside of the fish's mouth and was sticking out of its cheek. I backed away.

"Look, it's easy," said my father, ripping the hook out of the fish's mouth. My stomach turned. I wanted to be sick. He threw the fish into the ice chest and quickly closed the lid. "Good work son, one big, fat bass for dinner," he said, sitting down and picking up the paper. He caught two more fish, one on his line and one on mine, which I refused to reel in.

Soon after he caught his second fish, we packed up and got ready to go home. Before we left, nature called and my father disappeared into the bushes for a few minutes. Wanting to take another look at the fish, I opened the chest and peeked in. All three fish were lying on top of the ice, their silver scales glinting in the late afternoon sun. I closed the chest and sat on it. I gazed out at the lake. It was a crimson-tinted mirror in the setting sun. It was hard to believe that hundreds of fish were swimming around under that mirror. I wondered if our fish had brothers or sisters.

I stood up, opened the chest again, grabbed one of the fish and ran down to the water's edge. I threw the fish as far as I possibly could. I watched it tumble through the air and shatter the lake as it broke the surface. Then I ran back, grabbed the other two fish and threw them into the water too.

"What was that?" said my father, as he pushed through the bushes. I looked at the lake without answering. He followed my gaze, his eyes finally resting on the three fish floating on the surface some twenty yards from the beach. At first, my father didn't say anything. He picked up the chairs and poles and walked toward the car. He glanced over his shoulder and asked me to empty the ice out of the chest.

I took the chest down to the lake. It was so heavy I had to carry it with two hands. I opened the chest and tilted the ice into the water. The fish were still floating on the surface. I picked up the chest and ran back up the beach toward my father. Just before we got to the trees, I turned and took one more look at the lake. A sudden movement caught my eye. There was a ripple around the fish. I held my breath. Slowly, one of the fish rolled over, and with a lazy flap of its fin, disappeared under the surface. Within a few seconds the other fish followed. Then the ripples were gone and the lake became a mirror again.

I sat silent in the car on the way home. After a while, my father asked me if I was okay. On the verge of tears, I told him I wasn't sure. "I kind of feel bad," I said.

"Feel bad for those fish, huh?" he said.

"No," I said. "I feel bad about disappointing you." I kept my eyes out the window, not wanting to face my father.

"You didn't disappoint me," he said. He put his hand on my shoulder and told me that he reacted the same way I did when his dad took him fishing. He told me he still had a problem taking the hook out of a fish's mouth.

"Then why did we even take this trip?" I asked.

"Because, for ages, you've been talking about going on a fishing trip like other kids and their dads," he said. "I didn't want to disappoint you."

Sitting next to my father in that car is a moment I have always cherished, a special memory that supports and comforts me to this day. It was an incredible bonding experience, and the honesty and openness touched us both.

It was a great trip home.

10. The One-Legged Maniac

I often get invited to visit children's hospitals because of the work I have done with children suffering from childhood cancer. During one such visit to a children's hospital in Ohio, I met an amazing kid named Tylor Lauck.

I kept in touch with Tylor, and we wrote a book together about his journey with cancer. This kid was truly remarkable. Even through the most horrible bouts of nausea he still made mischief and created laughter everywhere he went. I called him the one-legged maniac because even though his leg was amputated, he still rollerbladed down the hospital halls on one leg and caused untold trouble for the nursing staff. He even once climbed a tree and got stuck!

Tylor was fading fast, and spent most of the time sleeping

on the couch. The evening before I was set to leave, family and friends sat around a huge bonfire outside Tylor's house. None of us said very much. We just stared at the flames and prayed silently for Tylor as he lay inside the house preparing for his final journey. Sparks floated above the fire and drifted ever upward, becoming indistinguishable from the stars in the clear night sky.

I was stirred from my thoughts when Tylor's uncle wondered if he could ask me a question. "Sure," I said.

"I hope you don't take this wrong," he said, "but why would you choose to spend time with a dying child? Why subject yourself to all of this pain and sadness if you don't have to?" A dozen grief-lined faces turned and looked at me expectantly.

"That's a good question," I replied. "I've asked myself that same question a thousand times." I stared at the fire again. The crackle of the flames added a comforting soundtrack to the night-insect symphony playing in the background.

"I guess kids with cancer have made me realize how great life is," I said. "They've shown me how lucky I am to be part of an incredibly vibrant and wonderful existence. This might sound silly, but I really feel great, almost elated, when I can make a sick kid laugh or when I'm able to comfort a hurting child...sometimes when nobody else can. It sounds crazy, but I've found very few things in the world that make me feel so worthwhile and fulfilled."

A gentle murmur and some slow, smiling nods acknowledged my sentiment. "I'll be honest with you," I said. "I get back way more than I ever give." Again we all stared at the fire without a word, listening to the hiss and crackle of the fire and the internal whispering of our own prayers echoing deep within our souls.

I got up and went inside to where Tylor's mom and dad were sitting alongside him as he lay on the couch. He had been lying there, unconscious, most of the day. "Hey T. Your buddy Trevor's here," his mom said, leaning over him and rubbing his head affectionately. Tylor's eyes fluttered open. Closed. Then opened again. With a trembling palm he reached out and patted my hand. Then he mumbled something I couldn't quite understand. I put my ear to his mouth.

"Love *yhh*," he said and closed his eyes again.

My heart felt like it wanted to burst with compassion for this great kid whose life was dangling on a flimsy thread. I leaned over and whispered in his ear, "I love you too, you one-legged maniac."

"That's me," he said. "And don't you forget it."

Tylor passed away two days later. Often when I close my eyes I see Tylor, in slow motion, patting my hand and I see his lips mouthing the words, "Love *yhh*." I feel both comfort and joy from having chosen to share so many laughs and tears with such a special young kid.

11. The Gift

I was attached to a contingency from the United Nation's Children and Armed Conflict division. We had traveled to the central African country of Burundi to help facilitate reintegration of former child soldiers into the community. I had worked with orphans in Africa before and thought I understood the plight of the children in the area. Before I left, I even spoke with Ishmael Beah, who wrote a memoir about his time as a child soldier in Sierra Leone. But I was still shocked by the state of the Burundian orphans I met. Burundi is one of the poorest countries in the world. A brutal twelve-year civil war left hundreds of thousands dead and even more displaced. There are hundreds of thousands of orphans from AIDS, from war, and from poverty.

But the thousands of child soldiers carry a unique burden. During the war, both sides took children as young as ten years old and forced them into frontline fighting. They saw the horrors of war firsthand and now faced mistrust and suspicion from their own people. It was hard to know what to say to them. The kids were sitting in a semicircle on a bunch of logs in a dusty courtyard when we drove in. I decided that I would simply visit with them and share some of my journal drawings and stories without pretending to know about how they might be feeling. I opened my heart, held my breath, and with the help of an interpreter, introduced myself.

I was tense at first but I quickly found out that my usual approach of using self-deprecating humor was a good way to connect. I said right away that I was a typical visitor who thought he knew everything about Burundian culture and that I was a skilled African dancer. "Watch this," I said. They looked at me like I was out of my mind as I got up and began doing a belly dance. They all laughed hysterically as I quickly sat down and covered my face. My actions broke the ice and before long I was having an intense and thought-provoking conversation with the kids.

We got onto the subject of hopes and dreams, and one of the boys told me that there was no hope for them. I asked him what he meant. "There are no jobs for us," he said. "There is no food. Our parents are dead. There is nothing. War was at least a job for us."

Everything was stripped bare in the compound. There wasn't a blade of grass in sight. I looked at the boy and picked up some dirt from around the crates we were sitting on. "Do you think anything can grow in this dirt?" I asked, letting the soil trickle through my fingers.

"No," said the boy.

"But, if you dig a little hole right here and plant a seed in the hole, will it grow?"

"No." said the boy, bluntly. "Nothing can grow in this dust."

"How about if you water the seed and take care of it every day?"

"It will grow," said the boy, smiling sheepishly.

"You know," I said, "back in America, I spend a lot of time with children who are very sick. They have a disease called cancer." I shared some stories about the brave children I have known over the years that have suffered from the disease. I told them that many of those kids get better, but some of them just cannot be cured, no matter how hard the doctors try. That for those kids there was no hope. "But for you," I said, "even after all the pain and terrible suffering you have experienced, I believe there are seeds of hope deep inside every one of you." The boys nodded and exchanged a few words to each other that I couldn't understand. "Guys, don't give up on your seeds. Love them, tend to them, look after them, treasure them and I bet you they will grow." Another murmur went up. Nods and more nods ensued. One of the boys leaned over and patted me on the knee. We sat in comfortable quietness for a few minutes.

Later I asked the kids what they loved the most. "Ice cream!"

they yelled. Apparently they had their first taste of ice cream the week before thanks to UNICEF. We spent most of the afternoon talking and sharing incredible stories. It was hard to leave those guys. They are such good kids stuck in such a tough place. As our convoy of white UN vehicles was about to leave the orphanage, one of the boys who had been in my group rushed up to the car window and thrust his hand inside. He was holding a soiled little pouch, which he dropped into my palm. I pulled the drawstring on the pouch and turned it over. A heavy, well-worn, antique Queen Victoria British coin, minted in 1890, tumbled out of the pouch into my hand.

"What is this?" I asked the boy.

"Please can you use it to buy ice cream for the children with cancer in the hospital," he said. I couldn't believe the compassion he expressed. He had nothing but the clothes on his back yet he gave what might be his only possession to help somebody else.

"Thanks!" I yelled as a cloud of dust enveloped the boy and all the others who had gathered at the gate to say goodbye. As we drove away, I turned and looked over my shoulder. The boy was still waving. I kept looking back until the boy became a speck on the horizon.

12. Comfort

I have spent many years working with children who are facing adversity, and people often ask me how I cope with the pain and suffering that I witness. They wonder how I recharge my own batteries and discharge the burden I carry away with me after working with them.

To relax, I exercise, and on most days you'll find me jogging around the lake where I live. Exercise really works to keep me going and helps reduce my stress. To stay centered, I spend as much time as possible drawing in my journal. Art has a meditative effect for me and really helps to clear my mind and open my heart.

But one thing I love is to play the guitar. Just messing around with tunes stirs so many wonderful thoughts and memories.

Sometimes old songs that I play help me to deal with current daily life by triggering comforting memories from my past. It's incredible how fast it can happen: one minute I can be sitting in my studio with my guitar playing a song from my youth, the next minute I can be back in my childhood room as a little boy—like the time I was playing my guitar and a chord brought back a memory of myself as a boy of nine or ten sitting in my bed in the middle of the night. I'm not sure what had woken me up, but I got scared and went to my parents' room to see if they were awake. If I was afraid at night, I would sometimes get out of bed and stand by the door of my parents' room just to hear them breathe. The slow, steady sound always soothed me.

That night, as I approached my parents' room, I noticed that the light was on in my dad's studio. I tiptoed up the stairs and peeked into the door. The glow of the desk lamp bathed the room in a warm light. My dad was hunched over his drawing board with his elbows on the table and his face resting in his hands. I didn't want to disturb him, so I just stood and watched. His radio was playing softly. The Mamas and the Papas were singing "California Dreamin'". I have always loved the opening chord from that song. Finally I cleared my throat. My dad looked up.

"Oh, hi Trev," he said, extending his arms toward me. As he wrapped his arms around me, I asked him if he was okay. "Just a lot to think about," he said. I knew that my dad was desperately trying to make a living as an artist, but we were struggling. It really hurt him that he could not support us like he wanted to. I asked if he was thinking about money. He sighed and ruffled my hair, pulling me close. "Couldn't sleep, huh?" Snuggling into his chest, wrapped in his arms, I felt safe and secure.

"Can I help?" I asked. I was saving for my very first guitar and I had a jar full of coins sitting on my windowsill. I would happily have given him every cent. I leaned back and looked into his eyes. I think I saw my father's soul through his eyes that night. He was always strong but I saw an endearing vulnerability that brought us even closer than we were.

"Yeah, you can help," he said, softly.

"How?" I asked.

"C'mere and hold me," he said, putting his arms around me again. I held my dad for the longest time.

13. Learning to Grieve from Elephants

The Timbavati Nature Reserve is located on the western boundary of South Africa's largest national park. The vast expanse of open savanna is home to an astounding variety of African wildlife, from rhinoceros to the exotic white lions that made the area famous. Created by conservationists, the unfenced reserve is meant to protect and maintain the animals and their environment.

When I was in school, we went on a field trip to the region. It was our last day in the park, and six of us were sitting in the back of an open Land Rover, with our geography teacher and the guide riding up front. The Land Rover was traveling toward our camp when the guide suddenly put on his brakes. The scrub and thorn bushes were very thick beside the dusty, hard-packed dirt road. We stood on our seats to enjoy the scenery, catching glimpses of a baboon, giraffes, and several varieties of gazelles and birds.

"Elephant," the guide said softly.

We all strained through the bush to see the elephant he was talking about. The bush was pretty thick and I could not catch sight of the animal. "Where, where?" we all whispered.

"Hang on," he said, swinging the wheel of the Land Rover. He moved the vehicle forward and pulled around a large clump of trees. A collective gasp rose though the air. Right in front of us was a magnificent old elephant. My heart started pounding. I had never been this close to an elephant before. The excitement and adrenaline that surged through my veins was suddenly countered by an awful nauseating revulsion. The bull elephant was prone. Lying on his side. With horror, I realized that he was dead.

"Damn!" muttered my geography teacher.

"Poachers," said the driver. The elephant's tusks were short and flat. The guide said they must have used a chainsaw. Murmurs of disgust filled the Land Rover. Suddenly the driver pointed. "Tula," he said, telling us to be quiet in Zulu. I followed to where he was pointing and saw another smaller elephant in the thicket standing and watching. Then I saw two others. They looked like they were crying. We all started whispering, wanting to do something.

"There is nothing we can do now," said the guide. He said he would radio the warden and let them know about the dead elephant, but the poachers were probably over the border in Mozambique by now. He said the rangers would come and get the meat for the villagers, so it wouldn't go to waste. "And the hyenas will clean the bones," he said. You could almost feel the sadness from the elephants. We felt helpless. The guide told us that the poachers would make more money from this one elephant than five years of salary. That as long as there is a demand for ivory, fur, and exotic animals, then the extermination would continue. The guide shook his head sadly. "The greed is creating the demand."

Suddenly, a movement from behind the dead elephant caught my eye. Again adrenaline surged through my body. It was a baby elephant, so small it had been hidden from our view by the body of the fallen bull. The baby moved into full view and seemed to be nudging the dead bull. "The dead one is probably the baby's grandfather," said the guide. "See how he is trying to wake him up." Silently, we watched the little baby elephant try to wake its grandfather. We could hear the little one whimpering as he tried again and again to rouse the bull that was at least ten times his size. The baby was making the saddest sounds I have ever heard, sounds that still haunt me when I think about them. The baby nudged and nudged the bull. Then he tapped the big elephant on the head, trying to get a reaction. The baby tried to push the elephant with his little head. It was heartbreaking. The baby was adamant and simply wouldn't give up.

Finally, two of the other elephants slowly came over and comforted the baby elephant. They touched the baby with their trunks and seemed to be stroking him in sympathy. The other elephants nudged the little one away from the bull, and with their ears and heads hanging, they moved slowly and deliberately off into the bush. The last thing I saw before they disappeared into the undergrowth was the baby elephant turn and gaze over its shoulder with a long, mournful look. I could swear the baby was crying. And then they were gone.

14. Action!

Named the uKhahlamba (the Barrier of Spears) by the Zulu people, the Drakensberg mountains are an imposing line of soaring fractured peaks in South Africa. The mountain range stretches for over 600 miles, and with its gaping valleys, scenic parks, and flowing waterfalls, is a place of stunning natural beauty.

I was lucky enough to visit the area while shooting a commercial for an advertising agency I was working for at the time. I loved agency work because it allowed me to work in places I might not normally have had the opportunity to visit. I had high expectations of this trip because I had visited the area before with my family as a child.

The local people were very accommodating and seemed to enjoy having us shoot a commercial there. There was always a group of fascinated adults watching us film and we had a resident group of kids who followed us around as we set up. The kids must have been around six or seven years old. Sometimes the crew got irritated with them and chased them off but I didn't mind the kids at all. I was actually inspired by their awe and interest in our work.

One young boy named Tuli was particularly fascinated with the process. He was very interested in what we were doing. Although he couldn't speak English, he indicated that he wanted to look through the camera. I loved his enthusiasm and let him stand on an apple crate to look through the lens.

This became a ritual. After setting up each shot, I would let him look through the lens. Then he'd step down and look at me.

"Action?" he would say.

"Action," I would reply nodding, and he would giggle heartily. Other than "hello, Mister," "action" was the only English word he knew. Tuli approved every single shot for me. We shot one scene on the banks of a mountain stream and I slipped on some moss-covered rocks and fell into the shallow water. I got completely drenched and banged up my arm. The first person to give me a hand was Tuli. He and his little group of buddies eagerly helped me up.

Afterward, I discovered that I had hit my watch on a rock and it had stopped working. At the end of the day we wrapped the shoot and I took off my broken watch. I was about to toss it in the trash when one of the African crewmembers stopped me and suggested I give it to one of the kids.

"But it's broken," I replied.

"Those guys can't afford watches," he said. I didn't know what the use of having a watch if you couldn't tell time. The crewmember chuckled. "We Africans don't use watches to tell the time. We rely on nature. We use the roosters to wake us up in the morning and a grumbling tummy tells us when it's time to eat. The watch for him will be a huge status symbol."

I still wasn't sure why someone would like a broken watch, but I took the man's advice and gave the watch to Tuli.

I'm glad I did. The look on his face was priceless. All the other kids rushed around him and ooohed and aaahed at his new watch. Seeing their joy and excitement over something I was going to throw away affected me deeply. I realized later it wasn't the watch that was important, but that I had acknowledged the existence of an enthusiastic little boy instead of chasing him away like the other crewmembers did.

We shot for the next few days, and every day, Tuli arrived proudly wearing his watch. As before, he approved each scene with a joyful exclamation of "action!" His approval must have helped because we garnered numerous awards for the commercial.

The commercial was so popular, that a few years later I went back to the region to shoot a sequel to the commercial. Lo and behold, who should appear but Tuli. Looking older and wiser, he still possessed his childlike enthusiasm as he smiled and hugged me in recognition. Again he followed the crew and approved every shot before we began filming. Every once in a while, I would ask him if he thought the lighting was good and the framing of the shot was okay. Sensing the joke, he would laugh and nod vigorously each time.

He came back the second morning of the shoot and approached me carrying a cloth in his hand. He unwrapped the cloth and in it was the watch I had given him years before. He looked up at me and grinned. I smiled back, patting him on the shoulder.

I keep that moment in a special place in my heart. The exchange is one of my favorite memories of all time.

"Yabonga," he said, thanking me in Zulu. Wrapping the watch carefully back into the cloth, he gently put it back into his pocket and smiled.

"Action?" he said, pointing to the scene we were about to shoot.

"Action," I nodded, and we walked toward the camera together.

15. Chico

When I met Chico, he was tied to a tree with a long chain. The chain was long enough for him to climb the tree trunk and sleep off the ground in the branches. He'd been captured on the Zimbabwe border and brought back to our base camp. I was fulfilling my service in the South African military at the time, and I confess that it was me who set Chico free.

Chico was a baboon and our army unit's mascot. Chico was a wonderful animal because he was affectionate and had a sense of humor that I liked to think was similar to mine. A number of us were opposed to Chico's capture, but our Staff-Sergeant considered Chico his pet and promised he would make life hell for anyone who released Chico for the remainder of their two-year service. The Staff-Sergeant was a tyrant and nobody wanted to be on his bad side, so we tried as hard as we could to make Chico happy. We often hung out with him and we enjoyed his hugs. He always tried to groom us and he loved to look through our pockets for change, which he'd grab and run off with.

We gave Chico a teddy bear to keep him company while we were away—sometimes for days—on maneuvers. Chico loved that tattered, overstuffed bear, and could often be seen nurturing and caressing it.

One day I brought Chico some leftover fruit from my dinner. As I approached his tree, I saw a group of new recruits taunting him; they were trying to get Chico to smoke a cigarette. Because I outranked the men, I told them to move along and not to let me catch them messing with the baboon again. This wasn't the first time Chico had been taunted and abused; the men often teased Chico.

I had guard duty later that night and my shift ended at 2 A.M. My friend Bruce and I walked past Chico's tree on our way back to our tent. It was pretty dark and we couldn't see Chico very clearly. I walked a little closer and suddenly realized that he was not alone: Chico and another baboon were huddled together at the base of the tree. It was so touching and heartbreaking to see the two of them holding each other like scared little children.

When the other baboon saw us it scampered off into the bush and I saw Chico look longingly after it. He then turned and looked at us. I thought about the Staff-Sergeant and his threats, but the sadness in Chico's eyes and the slight tilt of his head was all it took. My heart broke. I decided there and then to release Chico.

Bruce acted as a lookout while I approached Chico. The baboon backed away from me, probably thinking I was going to taunt him like the new recruits had done earlier that day. I stepped back and approached him again, this time crouching and softly whispering to him.

I got to Chico and reached out my hand. He took my hand and climbed onto my hip like he often did when we brought him fruit. I unhooked the chain from around his neck and walked away from the tree with him. He clung to me like a child, whimpering a little as I moved toward the edge of the clearing. It seemed like he did not want to go.

I put him down and without hesitation he scampered away from me toward the bush. Then he stopped, turned and ran back over to his tree where he'd been chained. Chico got to the tree and jumped up into the fork. Bruce and I frantically tried to shoo Chico to freedom, hissing at him to get away. Chico dug around for a few seconds and then dropped down to the ground and scuttled toward the undergrowth.

"Get out of here!" I urged.

As he neared the bush, he stopped and turned toward us. That's when I noticed Chico was carrying his teddy bear. I smiled to myself, now realizing why he had gone back to the tree. Way off in the distance, I heard an echo of the other baboon howling in the bush. Chico heard it too. He tucked the teddy bear under his arm, gave us one last chatter as if saying goodbye, and disappeared into the undergrowth.

16. The Climbing Tower

I love the sheer honesty and purity that kids have before they are influenced and molded by the world around them. Their innocence and clarity in dealing with life is uncomplicated and refreshing.

I once was a counselor at a camp for siblings of children with cancer. I led group D, a crew of eight children between the ages of eleven and thirteen. Each child was different. Each child was special. Each child had been through the harrowing wringer that childhood cancer drags families through.

The camp was located in a challenge-course arena, and our task that day was to scale a climbing wall sixty feet high. Each person had to wear a helmet and a harness when it was their turn to climb.

The first person to climb the tower was a boy named Andy, a wild thirteen-year-old who was going through the "you don't have to tell me nothin' because I know it all" stage. Andy was a loud, aggressive, and arrogant kid. To be honest, I did not like Andy very much. He was one of those kids who disrupted everything. He cussed all the time and was cocky. I'm ashamed to say that I would have preferred him not to be there.

Each child took their turn and slowly climbed this absurdly high wall, getting smaller and smaller the higher they went. Once they reached the top, they were to signal, then easily rappel down and celebrate with the other children when they reached the ground. Andy attacked the wall and climbed it in no time. On his way back down, his body language was cool and confident, looking down at us with a smirk that said he was a lot braver than we gave him credit for. "Hey, next time I wanna do it without that dumb harness," he bragged, once his feet were planted on terra firma.

Andy's brother Trey climbed next, also without any hesitation. Two of the girls in the group sat out the exercise because they were afraid of heights. A few kids got halfway up and decided to come down. I was due to climb last, and although I acted as though I didn't have a care in the world, I was beginning to get a little nervous about my impending climb.

Rebecca, an eleven-year-old, climbed up before me. Rebecca had lost her thirteen-year-old sister Jackie to cancer the year before. As one would expect, Rebecca was devastated by her sister's death. Jackie had been Rebecca's hero. She told me when Jackie died, it felt like there was a knife stuck in her heart, and she couldn't get it out.

Rebecca carried Jackie's death around with her, a heaviness that seemed to slow her movements. She often sat by herself and walked with slumped shoulders. I could tell she carried that burden with her as she climbed the wall. It was heavy going and she struggled a lot. She lost steam pretty quickly, and hovered on the rest platform that was situated about a two-thirds of the way up.

I was hooked up to the harness and climbed up alongside her. It wasn't easy. My whole body trembled as I clutched at those little wooden blocks and pulled myself up. I climbed alongside Rebecca and noticed she was crying. "C'mon, Rebecca, you can do it," I said.

"I don't think I can," she replied, sobbing. I decided to climb above Rebecca to see if I could help her up.

I heard the kids on the ground thirty feet below egging us on. That's when I made the mistake of looking down. I instantly felt faint and dizzy. Although I wanted to help Rebecca, all I could think about was myself. I wanted to be Mr. Cool Dude and didn't want to make a fool of myself in front of these kids—especially because I'd bragged earlier about how I had been in the army and this tower was nothing. To tell the truth, climbing that tower is one of the hardest things I have ever done in my life. I had made it to the top and wanted off as quickly as possible. I signed for the belay guide to release the rope so that I could rappel down.

As I rappelled down, I passed Rebecca. I was too worried about myself to stop and comfort her. The tower was bloody high and I was petrified! Rebecca's whole body was shaking as she clung to the tower. She was sobbing loudly. Rebecca's belay guide asked her if she could keep going.

"I don't think so," she sobbed.

Rebecca was just twenty feet from the top. She'd given it her best, but could not climb another inch. Her fingers, white at the knuckles, barely held on. She was crying so hard I could see her tears falling down and bouncing off the tower. We all stood back from the tower and yelled encouragement, but Rebecca seemed frozen. She couldn't go up and she couldn't come down.

Suddenly, Andy broke away from our group and went over to the foot of the tower. He put his hand up to his eyes to block the sun and squinted up at Rebecca. "Rebecca!" he yelled. "Rebecca!"

Rebecca turned and looked down at him standing below her at the bottom of the tower. "You can do it," he said. "Do it for your sister. Do it for Jackie!" The power of his suggestion seemed to stop time. Everything in the universe appeared to pause for a second. Sobbing uncontrollably, Rebecca heaved her body forward and began to climb. She did not hesitate. She climbed the last twenty feet with sheer heart and soul. When she reached the top she turned and looked down at us, the discovery of her inner strength was reflected joyfully on her face.

When she got down to the bottom of the tower, we all crowded around her and hugged her. Some of the kids cried with Rebecca. I did too. I will never forget the look of triumph and joy on Rebecca's face. Andy, who until then treated girls like the enemy and wouldn't dare touch one with an extremely long stick, sidled up to Rebecca and put his arm around her. "I knew you could do it," he said. He gave Rebecca a pat on the back and sauntered off to the cabins to get ready for dinner.

So often, we judge people on first impressions. I did not like Andy and wrote him off right from the beginning of camp. And yet, he did something really amazing for Rebecca, something I wasn't able to do.

At the time I did not realize how hard life was for Andy having a sibling in treatment. I just judged him by how much he was irritating me. Let me tell you, Andy is a great guy and I am ashamed of myself for not seeing past my first impression. Thank you Andy, for teaching me a great lesson.

17. Esther

Growing up, we had a nanny named Esther. She was, in essence, our second mommy. Esther was an incredible caretaker and it felt like Esther loved us like we were her own children. It seemed that she would do anything to protect us kids. This was indeed the case one afternoon when I was about five years old, while Esther and I were taking a walk in Johannesburg.

It was a beautiful afternoon, and Esther was holding my hand as we walked. The sky was a deep blue and the jacaranda trees were draped in a patchwork of purple blossoms. As we walked along the street we chatted with many of the maids who were sitting on the grassy sidewalks on their lunch breaks. Esther knew almost every person we passed on the street, and talked to them in their native Sotho. Even though I couldn't understand what Esther was saying, I loved to listen to their passionate chitchat. We were having a great afternoon. Then everything changed.

A yellow South African police van screeched to a halt beside us. Some of the maids started to run and two police constables jumped out of the van and started chasing them. Both policemen had *sjamboks* (whips) and they were hitting the petrified women. Esther and I watched in horror as the police rounded up five or six women, some we'd just been speaking to, and threw them into the back of the police van. Esther put her arms around me, shielding my eyes from the goings-on. Then she started slowly edging away from the van. I tried to look over my shoulder. "What are they doing?" I asked, bewildered.

"The maids don't have pass books," said Esther, turning my face away. "Come, we must go." Taking me by the arm, she repeated in Sotho, "Phakisa, phakisa" (*Hurry, hurry*). This was during apartheid. Blacks needed passes to be in white areas or they would be arrested. I remember protesting as Esther tried to pull me away. I said I didn't have a pass book either. "You are white," she said.

I was too young and didn't understand apartheid. I kept asking her to explain as she pulled me along. "I think it's because God forgot about us," she said, making a sign of the cross. Esther had left her pass at our house.

If God had forgotten about us, the constables didn't. "Hey you!" came a voice from behind us. It was one of the constables. "Stop!" Esther froze. It was my turn to pull her. I urged her to go. Esther grabbed my hand and started to run. One of the policemen yelled in Afrikaans, something I did understand. "I'm going to beat the hell out of you if you don't stop!" he said. Esther stopped and faced the policeman. The constable was a tall white man with a mustache and angry eyes. He yelled at Esther in Afrikaans, asking for her pass and calling her names. When he found out she didn't have it, he got louder and meaner.

When he told her to get into the van, I almost panicked. As if just noticing me, the policeman grabbed me by the collar and lifted me on to my tiptoes. He brought his face to within two inches of mine. His breath smelled bad. He told me to go home. I told him she was my nanny, and started to protest. The constable cuffed me upside the head and shoved me away. He had huge, rough hands with sausage fingers. I remember my ear stinging after he hit me.

"Leave him alone!" yelled Esther, trying to pull away from the grip of the second policeman." The constable grabbed Esther and half-pushed, half-threw her into the van. I saw her grimace as she scraped her knee on the threshold. The door slammed shut trapping Esther inside. "You can't leave this boy here by himself!" she shouted through the mesh bars. "He is only five years old. His house is far." The constables laughed and got into the van. "Go straight home!" yelled Esther out of the back of the van. "And cross the road by the light. Only when it's green." The van drove off leaving me standing on the sidewalk.

I lived almost seven blocks away and I ran all the way home and told my parents what had happened. My father had to pay a fine to get Esther out of the Norwood Police Station, which he did, and he brought her home. She had bruises on her arms and her legs from being hit with the sjambok. I hugged Esther so hard when she got back. I didn't want to let her go. I hid my face in the dark and comfortable folds of her dress, where I always found safety and solace as a young child. But no matter how hard I held her, I was still haunted by the look of pain and humiliation I saw on her face when the policemen threw her into the van. It never went away. Even today, I can still see it all clearly in my mind.

Esther died before I was old enough to understand and acknowledge how grateful I was for her unconditional caring. If I could, I would have thanked her from the bottom of my heart for taking care of me and protecting me when I was a vulnerable and scared little boy. Hers was a kindness I will never forget.

18. Prayer Beads

I didn't realize that the little elderly woman sitting next to me was praying, until I saw the mala (rosary prayer beads) in her hand. I thought she was speaking to herself, but she was, in fact, praying. I was sitting on a bench outside the Royal Orchid Hotel in Guam, waiting for a taxi to take me to the airport. I had just finished my USO tour doing stand-up comedy for kids on military bases on the island, and was getting ready to fly back to the United States. I was pleased with the visit, and felt like I really connected with the kids on the base.

The woman opened her eyes and caught me looking at her. I smiled and she smiled back.

"I pray," she said.

I nodded. "Can you tell God 'hello' from me?" I said.

"It's better if you tell him yourself," she said, handing me the string of beads. "His message machine is full." She patted my hands and smiled again.

I took the beads and closed my eyes. They were still warm from being clutched in her gnarled, worn hands. Picking up my internal phone, I dialed up the heavens and shared some moments of gratitude with my Maker.

While I was in that area code, I had a quick word with a number of friends and family who live in the same heavenly neighborhood. I spoke to my late father, my grandma, my grandfather, my childhood friend Howard who died while we were in the army, one of my favorite girlfriends, Babette, who passed away from an asthma attack, and Tylor, Vicki, Megan, Alex D., and some of the other kids I knew who died of cancer. Boy, it felt good to connect with them all. It is during rare quiet moments like this that I think about the people who have touched my life

While my eyes were closed I felt the old woman gently take the rosary. She patted my hands warmly. I smiled and a short time later opened my eyes. The woman was gone. I looked around but she was nowhere in sight. The seat beside me was empty but my heart was full.

I love meeting angels when I least expect to.

19. The Lady from KwaZulu

While on vacation with my mom a few years ago I met an incredible Zulu woman in KwaZulu-Natal, South Africa. She was a waitress at the hotel. The hotel was near the quiet seaside town of Salt Rock. It was a small, quaint, family-run hotel, overlooking the Indian Ocean. I was sitting under a thatch awning on the patio drinking a cup of tea and watching the dull, grey sea. The warm afternoon rain had sent most of the other guests indoors and she and I were the only people on the covered patio.

"I'm sorry it's raining," she said, pointing at the sea. "Is the rain spoiling your holiday?"

"No," I said, smiling. "I actually love the rain. It's very cleansing. I like to imagine the rain rinsing out my mind."

"Yebo," she sighed, using the Zulu word for *yes*.

She turned and stared out at the sea. Neither of us

said anything for a few minutes. We just looked out to sea, mesmerized by the breaking waves and the sound of the rain. I don't know what prompted me, but I turned to her and asked her if she was sad. She stood very still, looking out at the sea. After a moment she sighed. "Yebo," she said.

I looked at her and felt an overwhelming sense of compassion. She had tears in her eyes, and swimming in those tears I could sense a deep sadness. Even though it was probably against the rules, I pulled out a chair and invited her to sit. I poured some tea into my cup and handed it to her. She drained the cup and handed it back to me, thanking me politely in Zulu. She looked out to sea again.

"My husband, he passed away." she said, as if talking to the waves. "Last year. I was three months pregnant."

"I'm sorry," I said.

"Yebo. He died and after six months I had two boys. Twins. They were both dead when they were born."

I felt awful for this poor woman. I didn't know what to do. I wanted to hold her or give her money or run away—run away with shame because I was sitting like a king at the hotel being waited on by someone who should have been at home grieving for her husband and children instead of bringing me tea.

"I'm so sorry," I said again.

She pulled her attention from the waves. "Would you like another pot of tea?" she asked.

"No thanks," I said. "I'm fine."

She picked up the tray and walked toward the door of the hotel.

"Can I help you at all? Is there anything I can do?" I said.

She turned and smiled.

"You already did," she said.

20. Mother

Around my twelfth birthday, I discovered the art of photography. I would lie in bed as images and colors and thoughts of framing pictures just right kept me awake. My father had just lost his job, so there was no extra money for me to buy film or chemicals for developing my photographs. I understood the circumstances, so I hid my disappointment to save my parents from feeling any worse than they already did. There were absolutely no jobs to be had for kids my age, so there was no way for me to help the family, much less get money to buy film.

During that time, my mother began making little felt-stuffed dolls called Gonks. They were round, red characters with Beatle haircuts. One morning, I overheard my mom on the phone. She was in tears. I put my ear to the door like any twelve-year-old eavesdropper would do. Between her sniffles I heard my mom say that she only needed to sell a few more Gonks to have enough money to buy film and chemicals for me. "He is so passionate about photography," she said. "You should see his eyes when he talks about it." She said it broke her heart because she knew I was dying to take pictures. It was so comforting yet painful to know that my mother understood my passion for photography and would do anything to support me.

Two weeks later, my mom called me into my room and shut the door. She handed me a roll of film, some photographic paper, and chemicals. She asked me not say anything to anyone about it, especially my dad, because the money was needed elsewhere.

I was so excited I just wanted to burst. I hugged my mom, thanking her over and over again until she had to hush me. "I'll take great pictures for you, I promise," I whispered.

"Don't worry about taking great pictures for me," she said, a tear rolling down her cheek. "Just have fun."

"Mom, why are you crying?" I asked.

"Because I just love you so much." she said, ruffling my mop of curly hair. I connected with my mom that moment like I had never connected with her before. It was the beginning of a mutual appreciation for each other which continues to this day.

21. The Finding

During a trip to the Congo, I was privileged to visit the Don Bosco orphanage in Goma, a city that has been ravaged by war and almost destroyed by a nearby volcano. There were over 1,500 kids at the orphanage. The town itself is one of the poorest places I have ever laid eyes on; it was absolutely desolate—there were no paved roads, the buildings were ramshackle and falling down, and there were trenches on the side of the road that held sewage and wastewater.

Yet from the dust and volcanic ash grew an abundance of warmth and hospitality. The children and their caregivers living there welcomed me with songs, dances, and gratitude. I spent the day at the center working with various groups of kids. We discussed art, we discussed peace, and we discussed dreams. Even though the future seemed bleak for these children, it was amazing to see the sparkles of hope dancing in their eyes.

At one point in the afternoon, I felt a gentle tugging on my arm; I looked down to see a pair of big brown eyes looking up at me. The boy couldn't have been more that five years old. The interpreter said the boy wanted to ask me a question. I knelt down and looked into his beautiful eyes. Although they were bright and hopeful, I could tell that they had been washed time and time again with countless tears. I put my arm around the child and pulled him closer. He touched my face with his hand.

"Mister, can you help me find my mother?" he said. My heart froze because the interpreter, a teacher who worked at the orphanage, told me that both of the boy's parents had passed away. He asked again, "Can you help me find my mother?" I looked at the boy, my heart breaking, and tried not to panic. I didn't know what to say. How does one answer a question like that? I looked into my soul for an answer. And suddenly the words were there.

"Where do you think your mommy is?" I asked

"Oh, she's in heaven," he said quite comfortably.

"I'll tell you what," I said. "When I say my prayers tonight, I will ask God to pass on a message to your mommy. I'll ask Him to please tell your mommy that you send her your love and that you miss her. Okay?"

"Okay," he said, and he thanked me. I watched him skip off to play with a group of little boys who were kicking a ball nearby.

I realized that his caregivers were trying to protect him from the truth, but all the little guy wanted was for someone to listen to what he was asking for, instead of telling him what they thought he needed to hear.

22. The Old Man and the Bicycle

One of my favorite places in the world is the Drakensberg mountain range in South Africa. Referred to as the "Mountain of the Dragon" in Afrikaans or "Barrier of the Spears" by the Zulu people, it is a magnificent semicircular mountain range between the KwaZulu-Natal province of South Africa and the inland mountain kingdom of Lesotho. I have never been to the region without being totally awed by the spectacular scenery and dramatic views.

It was during a weekend trip to the area that I met the old man. I was driving along and enjoying the spectacular view with my girlfriend, Jenny, when we noticed him on a bicycle, slowly pedaling toward us up the hill. I slowed to a crawl so as not to shower him with dust. The man looked to be in his seventies or eighties. I waved out of the window and greeted him in Zulu, "Sawubona" [*hello*].

"Sawubona umugane," [*hello friend*] he replied, flashing me a wide toothless grin. He wobbled unsteadily on his rickety old bicycle, but still managed to wave.

A few seconds later, a pickup truck sped towards us from the other direction. Swirls of dust and dirt spewed out from behind the fishtailing vehicle. The pickup was full of rowdy teenage boys who yelled at us as they went by. I watched them in my rearview mirror and was horrified to see them aim directly for the old man on the bicycle. The driver swerved at the last second, enveloping the man in a cloud of dust. He teetered on the bike and finally fell into the brush alongside the road.

I turned my car around and went back to see if he was okay. He seemed to be fine, albeit a little shaken. His bike was not so lucky. The front wheel was totally bent and buckled. The old man looked so sad. "Haai eh-eh," he said, shaking his head. "What is wrong with those kids?" I popped the man's bicycle into the trunk of the car and we took him to the hotel where he worked. I asked if he wanted me to take him to a doctor but he said he was fine, just that his "happy place" was bruised.

As we we're leaving, I gave the man about eighty rand in cash that I had in my wallet and a few rand Jenny had in her purse. It was barely fifty US dollars. "It's to fix your bike," I said.

"I can't take your money," he said.

"Nah, it's okay," said Jenny. "He would have spent it on beer anyway and that's not good for that stomach of his."

The old man chuckled and told me I had a wise girlfriend. "I must pay you back," he said. I told him it was okay but he insisted, so I gave him my address. Jenny and I continued on our trip, and thoughts of the old man and his bike drifted toward the back of my mind and hung out with many other experiences that were hoping to be retold sometime in the future.

The battered and scuffed envelope arrived at my apartment exactly one month later. In the envelope was one very crumpled and tattered one-rand note and twenty-five cents. It was from the old man. One month later, another envelope arrived with a one-rand bill and twenty-five cents in it. No note, no return address, just the money the man was repaying. Religiously, an envelope arrived each and every month without fail.

Almost a year later, I happened to go back to the Drakensberg Mountains to shoot a television commercial. The filming took place very close to where we had met the old man, and I decided to look him up and thank him for being true to his word. I also wanted to tell him that it was really fine for him to stop sending me money every month.

I discovered that he had retired from the hotel and I was directed to his hut in a nearby contoured, thatch-roofed village that hugged the side of the hill near Champagne Castle. The huts in the village were made of mud and had dirt floors. I found out later that the people living in the village were exceptionally poor and barely able to make ends meet. As I knocked on the door I noticed that the windows were covered with cardboard and that there was no glass. A very old lady with a bent frame and a cane opened the door and smiled as I introduced myself.

I asked for the old man and I was sad to hear that he had passed away a number of months before. I also discovered that the woman who opened the door was his wife. She was the sweetest old lady you could imagine and was still repaying her husband's debt, sending me one-rand twenty-five every month even though he had died. I told her not to worry, that the money was just a gift, and to please keep it for herself. She was very thankful. I gave her a little more money, and got back into my car. As I drove away, I gave thanks for having the good fortune of having met such humble, good people.

In my life, I can only hope to have a fraction of the integrity, honesty, goodness and sincerity that the old man and his wife had. There is an apt Zulu phrase that always reminds me of them: "Iganekwane qhubeka funzelela phambili." *May their goodness survive and continue to inspire.*

23. Fishing in Guantanamo Bay

I had the honor of visiting Guantanamo Bay, Cuba, recently, where I was doing a stand-up comedy tour with the USO for the kids on the base. It's particularly tough for the military kids living in Guantanamo Bay—there are only a few restaurants, a couple of stores, and an outdoor movie theater. There is not much for the kids to do there and they cannot leave the base, except for short fishing and boating excursions around the bay.

The USO not only works exceptionally hard to serve the men and women in the Armed Forces; they also serve the entire military family. I am proud to be part of the USO's extensive efforts to help make the lives of military children easier, especially those whose parents are deployed or away from home.

While I was in Guantanamo Bay, I stayed at the Bachelor Officer Quarters, which is right on the water. As one would imagine, the waters of the Caribbean are a stunning turquoise color. The morning of my show, I was sitting on the pier near where I was staying, totally mesmerized by the water. Voices in the distance filtered into my brain and I looked up to see a father and his two sons on a small boat floating nearby. It was wonderful to see the boys with their father, who was lovingly teaching the younger boy how to fish. From the snippets of conversation that reached me across the water, I was able to discern that this was the first fishing trip for the younger boy and that his dad was going to be deployed in the near future.

I'd gone back to daydreaming when I suddenly heard a shriek. The boy was frantically reeling in his line. To his utter surprise and delight, he lifted his fishing pole and there was a good-sized fish on the end of it. I watched as the boy's father and brother both praised him for his first catch and helped him get the fish off the hook and into the boat.

The boy marveled at the fish, holding it tightly like his father told him to. "Hello?" said the boy, putting his face right up to the fish's mouth. I could see the fish and the boy stared at each other face to face. Then the fish suddenly nipped the boy's nose. In shock, the boy reeled back and let go of the fish. It bounced off the seat and flipped back into the water. They all looked stunned.

The father raised his eyebrows and lifted his finger as if to say something, but all at once the three of them burst into peals of laughter. It was wonderful to see them hugging and laughing in the boat. The echo of their joyous giggling wafted across the water and tickled me too. I chuckled with them from a distance, enjoying the love and affection the father was sharing with his sons before his deployment.

It was so nice to see a father so close to his children, because lately, I have seen and heard so many stories from all around the world about absent dads and abandoned kids. It was encouraging to see this dad spending meaningful time with his kids before leaving for an extended period of time. I have similar memories of moments spent with my own father. Those memories prop me up and sustain me when I'm feeling down.

I watched them in the boat, their heads thrown back as they laughed and laughed long after the fish was gone, and I hoped that this experience, like the memories I have of the great times with my father, would stay with the boys for years to come, and comfort them while their dad was deployed. The pleasure of their laughter drifted happily on the breeze as they paddled away, and it stayed long after they disappeared in the distance.

24. Grace

Several years ago, I was invited by the United Nations to work with children in refugee camps in the Democratic Republic of the Congo and Burundi. During my visit I had the privilege of sharing art and stories with a group of orphans at the Don Bosco Youth Center in the North Kivu town of Goma.

The only person who could speak English in the group, including the teacher, was Grace, a nineteen-year-old Congolese woman who worked as an aide at the center. She had a wonderful sense of humor and made it very easy for me to share a laugh with the kids in the classroom.

At the end of the day, I sat on a box near the center's buckled tin gate, waiting for my ride. Apparently, there had been a spot of trouble in town with a roadblock, and the driver who was supposed to come and fetch me had not yet arrived. As I waited, I watched the sun setting over the poverty-stricken landscape. Ravaged by four decades of civil war that had only just ended, and still devastated by a volcano from six years before, it was a forlorn and desolate place. The sun looked like a big red ball as it slowly rolled through the dust-covered sky and over the edge of the horizon.

After several hours of waiting, I started to worry about how I was going to get back to the UN compound, which was some seven miles away. The area was still occupied by a number of hostile rebel soldiers and was considered dangerous. I decided to stand on the box and peer over the fence to see if I could spot the white UN vehicle that was supposed to come and get me.

"You shouldn't do that," a concerned voice called from behind me. It was Grace, the young lady who translated for me during the day. I quickly got off the box.

"Jambo," I said, using in the Swahili word for "hello."

"Jambo Mr. Trevor," she said. "I came to tell you that you shouldn't do that."

"Do what?" I replied. Now that I was off the box, she relaxed and smiled.

"Put all of your good ideas in big danger like that," she grinned.

"What do you mean?" I asked, confused.

"Well. I know from working with you today that there are many good ideas in your head." I shook my head, still not sure what she was talking about. "You see," she said, "if you stand on the box and put your head over the fence like that, then somebody is going to shoot your head. And if they shoot well there will be a hole in your head and all the ideas will fall out. That is not good."

"No it isn't," I said, laughing and thanking her. Even though I had passed the United Nations "Security In The Field" course, the reality on the ground was far different. Hearing that one should not put oneself into places that might draw attention is one thing. Knowing when to duck stray bullets from drunken ex-rebels and warlords looking for target practice is quite another.

"You cannot sit alone," she said. "It is our custom to look after our guests." So we sat together, and I asked Grace to tell me about life in the Congo. She spoke with an openness and candor that I've grown to recognize in those coping with adversity. She had suffered terrible trauma yet seemed calm and rather philosophical. She told me that three of her younger siblings and her father had been killed in the war. She hinted that bad things had happened to her as well. I asked about her hopes and dreams for the future, and she told me that she wanted to go to school one day to be a nurse, but as she was the family breadwinner, it was a struggle to save money for college.

Two hours later the UN driver finally arrived and I hugged Grace and thanked her for staying with me. I wanted to give her something as a token of my appreciation and the only thing I had on me was a twenty-dollar bill. Twenty dollars would be at least two months' salary for the average earner in the Congo. "This is for you," I said, I handing her the money.

She looked at me and shook her head. "Thank you, but my father always told me I must earn my money," she said. "If I get money because people feel sorry for me, then the devil inside my head will trick me into trying to look for more money that same way." She smiled, handing me the money back. "And then I will forget how to work for my dreams," she said.

As we drove away from the orphanage, I replayed what she said, impressed with her deep insight and a wisdom well beyond her years. What an honor to share time with such an inspiring person. I fiddled with the twenty-dollar bill in my pocket and I thought, "How many times do I have to be reminded that it's not about the money?"

25. Quiet Comfort

A good friend of mine told me a touching story. We were chatting about my book, *What On Earth Do You Do When Someone Dies?* and she told me that one of her neighbors lost a child last month in a drowning accident. She told me she was afraid to visit the woman because she didn't know what to say to her. Apparently, her nine-year-old daughter didn't hesitate and went right across the road.

When she got back, my friend asked her daughter what she had said to the devastated mom.

"I didn't say anything," said the girl. "I just sat on her lap and we cried."

26. Mr. Wemba

Kinshasa is one of the most visually overwhelming cities I have ever visited. It looks like a war zone filled with burnt-out buildings, tin shanties, and potholes filled with stagnant water. There are throngs of people everywhere you look. It's the capital of the Democratic Republic of the Congo situated in Central Africa. It is also home to more than seven million people, and hosts one of the largest slums in the world. But while I was there, I did have the privilege of meeting a wonderful man named Mr. Wemba.

I was in Kinshasa to meet with the United Nations and UNICEF, and was invited to visit a clinic for abused women. Most of the women in the clinic, including the nurses, had been raped or abused. After listening to their heartbreaking stories, one after another, I had to take a moment and step outside.

One of the ways I calm myself is by sketching in my journal, so I opened my journal and looked around at the crumbling, broken-down buildings and the forlorn corrugated-tin shacks for something to catch my eye. The stench matched the nauseating sight of old tires, rusted tin cans, cardboard boxes, abandoned vehicles, and other rubbish that lay heaped against people's homes. There was dirt and filth piled everywhere. Discarded plastic bags and scraps of paper danced a somber ballet in and around the structures. As I looked around trying to make sense of what I was seeing, a patch of yellow caught my eye. The color was totally out of place. I beckoned our UN driver over and we walked toward the splash of color.

"I think it's somebody's house," the driver said, as we got a little closer.

We stepped around a rusted-out VW bus and there, nestled between the broken-down, mangled, and filthy tin shanties was a yellow corrugated dwelling with purple and green accents. It was a sight to behold. This little house was made out of tin and wood, like the others surrounding it, but it was immaculate.

Even the immediate area around the house was clean-swept and beautiful. A magnificent flowerbed filled with colorful blooming plants embraced the front and sides of the house. Also on the sides were dozens of old paint cans filled with flowers. Under the window, which was actually a plastic-covered hole in the wall, was an old commode filled with soil and a beautiful hibiscus tree. It was like a perfect rose growing in amongst coils of rusted barbed wire.

As we were standing there, a man stepped out of the house and introduced himself as Mr. Wemba. I apologized for staring and told him his home was beautiful. He thanked me graciously, and pointed to the unkempt houses around him, saying his neighbors weren't very happy with him. "They say I am making them look bad." He laughed heartily. "Well what can I say?"

As we talked, I told him that I was from South Africa. Mr. Wemba nodded sagely. "Your grandfather is a good man," he said.

"How do you know my grandfather?" I asked.

"Nelson Mandela," he said, "is the grandfather of all South Africans."

"Yes indeed. Madiba is a wonderful human being," I said, using the name Nelson Mandela is known by in South Africa. We chatted a little more about the Congo, life in Kinshasa, and how much work was needed to give the children hope for the future. I told him I was with a UN delegation trying to help children affected by the war.

Mr. Wemba gave a long sigh, shaking his head. "I believe that would mean every child in the whole country," he said.

A few minutes later we waved our goodbyes and I watched him go back into his lovely home, that solitary bright patch of color and flowers amongst gloomy broken-down shacks. It's amazing how some people are inspired to use anything and everything in their power not to become part of the fabric of their surroundings and situations. Standing there, I made a wish for the children in the slums, orphanages, and refugee camps in Africa—for there to be an abundance of Mr. Wembas helping kids grow and blossom despite being surrounded by war, poverty, and famine.

27. Jam Jar

I grew up in Johannesburg, South Africa, and most families at that time had a nanny who took care of the young children in the household. Our nanny's name was Esther. Esther was a warm, cuddly Sotho woman who had the most amazing ability to soothe children, no matter what the circumstances. She was a great comforter, especially after I had fallen off my bicycle or was scared by something in the dark.

One summer afternoon, I was in my room sketching in my journal when I heard Esther speaking to her mother in the backyard. I could tell something was wrong by the tone of Esther's voice. I climbed onto my bed and peered through the lace curtains. Esther and her mother were sitting under my window on wooden crates, drinking tea and talking.

The talking stopped a few minutes later, and then I heard Esther sobbing. I rushed outside and asked Esther what was wrong. Her mother was comforting her and stroking her arm. Esther was like a second mother to me and it upset me to see her crying. I ran over to her and leapt into her lap like I always did, almost spilling her tea.

"Esther, what's the matter?" I asked.

"It's nothing, my boy," she replied, ruffling my hair. "It's time for your bath. You must go inside now; otherwise, your daddy and mommy will be cross."

"But what's wrong?" I asked again.

"I told you, it's nothing," said Esther, smiling.

"But you're crying," I said.

"It's not so bad," she replied. "I am just a little worried about money. Now hurry up and bathe."

The pay for nannies at that time was appallingly low and Esther was no exception. I went inside and headed straight for my secret hiding place behind the French dresser in the living room. I put my hand into the tiny cubbyhole in the back and retrieved my jam-jar piggy bank. I was quite rich for a six-year-old. I remember I had exactly three rand and twenty-eight cents in the jar. I unscrewed the lid quietly and emptied the jar. I went back outside and rushed up to Esther again.

"I know, I know, I have to bathe," I said. "But I wanted to give you one last hug." I hugged Esther and slipped the money into the pocket of her work dress. I went to bed that night feeling very pleased with myself.

The next afternoon there was a huge thunderstorm. Storms

in Johannesburg are truly spectacular—they don't normally last very long but they are intense and powerful. The thunder booms violently, rumbling angrily across the highveld. And because of the altitude, dry air, and location, lightning almost always lights up the sky during a storm. During that storm, I hid behind the dresser for safety, like I always did. I sat there until my mom peeked her head over the top and said, "It's okay Trev, you can come out. The storm is over." As I climbed out from behind the dresser, I glanced into the cubbyhole that housed my jam-jar piggy bank. I stopped. There was something in the jar. I opened the lid and found three rand and twenty-eight cents inside...plus a single English Toffee: my favorite candy of all time.

28. Hazel Eyes

Back when I worked in advertising, I directed a television commercial in Lesotho, a mountainous country sitting completely within the borders of South Africa. The Lesotho highlands where I was filming are a rugged spectacle of remote villages nestled around deep valleys below tall mountain peaks.

I couldn't resist the natural beauty of that place, and during the inevitable downtime during the commercial shoot, I convinced a cameraman who was a friend of mine to drive me along the mountain roads so that I could take some pictures. Every time we stopped to take a picture, local kids came rushing out of the small villages to greet us. It was rare for them to see visitors, and on my outings I always made sure to carry a big bag of goodies to hand out to the kids, including candy and fruit, because they were so impoverished and didn't often get treats.

At one particular stop I photographed almost ten kids. They were from a small group of round, thatch-roofed mud huts and had chased the car for a half a mile before I noticed them yelling and waving from the cloud of dust behind the vehicle. Even though they were barefoot and wore old, tattered clothes, they smiled broadly when they caught up to us. After handing out a bunch of candy and some bread and fruit, I sat on the hood of the car and reloaded my camera with a new roll of film. A movement from a huge thorn tree just off the road caught my eye. I looked over and noticed a young girl peering out from behind the tree. When she realized I had spotted her, she quickly ducked back behind the tree.

"Tell her to come and get some goodies," I said to the cameraman. He spoke the local language and called her over, but she stayed behind the tree. I held up the bag of candy. She didn't budge. I slowly got off the hood of the car and walked over to the tree holding out the bag. My friend walked with me. I extended my hand to the girl and she reached around the tree and without showing her face took a handful of sweets. "Don't be afraid," I said, and my friend translated. The girl spoke timidly with eyes downcast from behind the tree.

"She says she is afraid you will be scared of her," he said.

"Why should I be scared of her?" I asked. He relayed the question. The girl answered.

"She says you will be afraid because she is ugly," he replied.

"That's ridiculous." I said. "Tell her I'll show her that she's not ugly." He spoke to the girl and after a lot of banter and coaching he talked her out from behind the tree. I caught my breath as the girl came into full view. She was beautiful, with dark hair and dark skin and the most amazing hazel eyes.

"Ah ha! She is hiding because of her eyes," said my friend. He explained that very few Africans have green in their eyes. He guessed that her village's witch doctors thought she was evil and would bring people bad luck. That's probably why she was alone, not playing with the other kids. He spoke to her again. She replied without looking at him. "The elders have kicked her out of the village," he said. "They won't let her come near the huts. She lives in the back where the chickens sleep."

"That's so sad," I said.

"We are a very superstitious people," he said, grinning. "Things like that are considered a sign from the gods."

"Tell her I want to show her something beautiful," I said. As he translated, the girl looked at me shyly. Then my friend said something and she smiled.

"What did you say to her?" I asked.

"I told her you wanted to show her something beautiful." He replied. "Then I told her not to worry because the only ugly thing around here was you, not her, because you are so white."

We burst into laughter.

"Am I really ugly?" I asked him.

"A little," he replied. We both laughed again and this seemed to put the girl at ease.

I took out my Polaroid camera and positioned myself in

front of the girl. She leaned forward and peered curiously at the camera. I took the picture and the photograph popped out of the camera. The picture captured the girl's beauty perfectly.

"You are very beautiful," I said, and handed her the picture. She held the picture like it was the most delicate thing she had ever handled in her life. She stared in amazement for the longest time.

It was evident that she had never seen a picture of herself. "Is this me?" she asked, pointing to herself. We nodded. The little girl glanced up and said something to my friend. I asked him what she said.

He looked like he was about to cry. "She said, 'You are right. I am beautiful'."

29. You're Not Here But You're Always There

He reached under the bed and pulled me out.

"Are you okay?" he asked.

"No," I replied.

"What's wrong?" he said, putting his arm around me.

"I miss you, Dad," I said.

"I miss you, too," he said.

"I wish you were still alive," I sighed.

"But, I'll always be in your heart," he said softly.

"I know," I replied. "But I still miss you."

"I feel the same," he said.

"Is this a dream?" I asked.

"Unfortunately, it is," he smiled.

"Why am I a little boy when I dream about you," I asked, "not the age I am now?"

"Because you're my little boy," he said, holding me tightly. "And you always will be."

Even though my father is gone, he taught me the art of caring, and still remains a guiding light in my life.

30. The Nee Nee Man

When I was a young boy, there was a gray-haired old African man who walked the streets of Johannesburg, spreading what he called "God's Joy." He always carried a ragged, brown, leather suitcase and wore a red fez on his head. And even though he was poor and his shoes were worn totally through, he had a genuine, infectious grin. He would graciously hand out incense to people who stopped to hear him sing his song.

He always chanted the same song: "Na nee, nee, nee. Na nee, nee, nee." He did this over and over again as he walked. That's why everybody called him the Nee Nee Man. We would get so excited when we saw him walking down our street. Kids in the neighborhood would run out of their houses when they heard him singing. He was funny and magical and seemed so joyous, it was always good to see him.

The Nee Nee Man walked hundreds of miles every week

spreading his word and handing out incense. As a kid, I saw him all over Johannesburg as I peered over the edge of the window in the back seat of my father's car. He walked for years and years. For a long while I didn't see him—wondering worriedly if he was okay—but he appeared again when I was in my final year of school.

He came into the sandwich shop where I was working during a school vacation. "It's the Nee Nee Man," I said, happily welcoming him into the store. "What can I get you?" I asked, smiling at the man in the red fez who brought my own happy youth back to visit me through his eyes.

"I'll just have some water," he said. "I have no money for food." I gave the Nee Nee Man some water and a sandwich on the house. He appeared again the next day. And the day after. He walked through a very happy time in my childhood and I felt compelled to give him a free sandwich each time I saw him. "Thank you," said the Nee Nee Man. "I will pay you back one day." I told him the smiles he gave me as a kid were more than enough payment. This happened every day for about three weeks.

One day, the owner of the deli asked me to drop off the morning's profits at the bank on my lunch break. I took the bank bag with the money in it and left the shop, heading down the street to the bank. I was walking down Rissik Street, a busy thoroughfare, when I noticed four shady-looking characters loitering on the sidewalk in front of me. Something was not quite right about the way they glanced at me. Too late, I realized that I was walking with the bank bag out for anyone to see. I quickly crossed the street and turned a corner. Before I made it to the next block, the men appeared from an alley in front of me.

They sauntered along very slowly towards me. My heart began beating very quickly and I got scared. It was too late to run. I braced myself for a confrontation when suddenly, the Nee Nee Man appeared out of nowhere.

He strode directly toward the group of slouching men. They stopped, shuffling to hide behind one another. The Nee Nee Man pointed his finger and yelled at them in Zulu. The men's eyes grew big and they cowered at his voice. They backed away and dispersed in different directions.

The Nee Nee Man smiled at me. "Don't worry. They won't bother you again," he said, patting me on the shoulder. Before I could thank him, before I could say anything, he walked off down the street. I watched him go, listening to him sing that song from my childhood, "Na nee, nee, nee. Na nee, nee, nee."

31. Painting on a Hundred-Year-Old Canvas

Art has always been a part of my life. I've worked in many mediums, including watercolor, acrylic, markers, and colored pencils. I've worked on murals, painted on walls, and sketched in countless notebooks. A few years ago, I had the distinct privilege of painting on a hundred-year-old canvas. This canvas imparted some of the most inspiring tales and truths I have ever heard. In spirit, many canvases have whispered ideas to me, but this was the first time a canvas had ever actually spoken to me. To tell you the truth, it was the first time I had ever painted on a canvas that was actually alive.

The canvas was Bess Wilson, a one-hundred-year-old friend of our family. By calling Bess a canvas, I am not implying that Bess has rough skin—on the contrary, she is the quintessential

Oil of Olay girl. Bess did not look one hundred years old. Her eyes still sparkled, she was very energetic, and looked at least twenty years younger than she was.

The way it happened was quite sweet, really. Her nails were in bad shape and she needed them painted. I volunteered. Hey, painting is painting, right? I had never painted nails before, but I love to learn, so I painted Bess's nails while she spoke about her life.

What an honor to hold her thin, soft, loving fingers and paint the nails on hands that have seen a hundred years go by. Hands that have been wrung for the death of two husbands and her only son. Hands that held the wheel of a Model T Ford. Hands that begged for scraps during the Depression. Hands that bled while picking cotton in Alabama. Hands that held an amazing new invention called a transistor radio. Hands that held a stillborn child. Hands that prayed during World War I, World War II, the Korean War, the Vietnam War, the death of President Kennedy, and the fall of the towers at the World Trade Center.

"I've seen a lot," Bess told me after I had finished painting her nails. "But seeing a grown man painting a hundred-year-old lady's nails, now that's something I have never seen." She clasped my hands in hers and thanked me. "You made me very happy today," she said. "This is something I will remember, unless I forget it when I get really old."

32. Cartoon Man

The art teacher at my high school was not fond of pen and ink cartoon illustrations. As far as I was concerned, any art was fine by me, but he said that line art was not fine art and was a waste of time, as far as he was concerned. My teacher went so far as to tell my father that I was not talented enough to continue studying art as an elective in high school. Because of that teacher, I stopped drawing for almost twenty years.

But I loved line drawings, and continued to appreciate and collect pen and ink cartoons and sketches. It was pen and ink that I used when I started drawing again in my thirties. And it was my love for cartoons and line drawings that saved me from big trouble in the Congo.

I was in a car with a United Nations driver on my way from

an orphanage to a camp for ex–child soldiers. We were in the middle of nowhere, driving on a dirt road with fields on either side, when we suddenly came over a rise and the car screeched to a halt. Right in front of us was a red and white barrier blocking the road with a little wooden guard post on the side. The post was watched by two armed men in combat fatigues who could have been Congolese soldiers or rebels.

One soldier carried an AK-47 and the other casually held an old rusted rocket launcher with a dented and scratched grenade attached. They both wore berets and sunglasses and had belts filled with ammunition strung across their chests like Mardi Gras beads. Although I was with a United Nations driver, I was more than a little nervous because of many horror stories told by people working in the area.

The guy without the rocket launcher sauntered over to the car and peered in the window. "Where are you going?" he asked gruffly, his rifle slightly raised. I told him we were going to Don Bosco, the children's center, to work with the children there. "What work?" he asked.

"I'm helping the kids. You know? Stress from the war?" I said.

He looked at me suspiciously. "The war is finished," he said. I started to explain about post-traumatic stress but he stopped me and asked me for my papers. I gave him my UN passport and my clearance papers. He walked slowly back to the guard post and conferred with the other soldier. I started to get a little more worried when it appeared that the two men were arguing.

After what seemed like an eternity the soldier slowly walked back to the car. "Where are you going?" he asked again.

"Ummm...as I said, we're going to Don Bosco."

"Why?"

"To work with the kids," I said, smiling.

"What work?" There was a dangerous edge to his voice this time. The driver sat stiffly, not moving. It felt like the situation could take a very bad turn at any moment. Just then, I remembered some advice that my dad once told me: Kill them with kindness.

"Look," I said, giving the soldier a respectful smile. I opened my journal, which was filled with cartoon characters, sketches, and illustrations. The soldier leaned into the window and peered at my journal as I flipped the pages.

"You draw this?" he asked, pointing at the journal. I nodded. "You draw me?"

"Okay," I said. I turned to a blank page and looked up at him. He suddenly jumped to attention and saluted me with a big grin. He held the pose while I sketched. After I was done, I lifted the book and showed him the picture.

"Cartoon Man," he said. He flashed me an approving smile and the tension disappeared. I tore the picture out of the journal and handed it to him. He waved at the other soldier, calling him over to show him the picture. "Come!" he yelled. "Cartoon Man!" The other soldier rushed over. Seconds later I found myself sketching the other soldier, who also saluted me while I drew. I gave him the picture and they both marveled at their drawings. They accepted the sketches with a surprising joy and enthusiasm, giggling like a pair of school kids, comparing their pictures, and laughing at how I captured them on paper. With a big thumbs-up, followed by a serious salute and one last "Cartoon Man!" they lifted the barrier and we drove to Don Bosco.

The next day we drove along the same road and found the barrier across the road once more. With a scowl, one of the soldiers approached the car. He suddenly recognized me, jumped to attention and saluted me. "Cartoon Man!" he yelled, and signaled for the other soldier to let me through.

The other soldier lifted the barrier, yelled "Cartoon Man!" and happily waved me on.

33. The Light

I have spent time with many sick children, a lot of them suffering from cancer. Many of the kids survive; some of them don't. It's amazing that the children who succumb to the disease seem to know that they might not make it. Even when they have realized this, they almost always live their lives to the full to the very end. Vicki was no exception. She lived every single day to its full potential. Vicki was a beautiful fourteen-year-old and always had aspirations of being a model. As much as cancer and chemotherapy tried to smudge her beauty, they failed to succeed.

When I realized she was close to the end of her life, I thought her dream of being a model would probably not come true. Or would it? I called my friend Randal, a professional photographer who'd worked with top models on advertising campaigns for years. I told Randal the situation and asked him if he could help. Randal came to meet Vicki and was blown away by her beauty. He was visibly moved after visiting with her and agreed wholeheartedly to photograph her.

We brought the photographic equipment to the hospital and turned Vicki's room into a real photographic studio. There were wires and lights and cameras and reflectors and people all over the room. Vicki's excitement was contagious. Here was a child, hooked up to machines, totally nauseated from chemotherapy, and still running the show, making sure that nothing in the world was going to take the moment from her.

In the middle of the photo session, a nurse came in to give Vicki a round of medicine. The picture-taking was interrupted while Vicki was medicated through a tube that went directly into her heart. The nurse wasn't very happy that day and her attitude reflected it. Vicki, playing the diva, said, "Excuse me. Mind leaving your bad mood outside?" Vicki's mom and I laughed so hard we almost collapsed. Even the nurse cracked a smile.

Sometimes when I feel grumpy or down and find myself taking it out on other people, I think of Vicki. She had every right in the world to be miserable and downright depressed, but she always found time to smile and make the most of the moment.

"I hope thousands of people will get to see your picture," I said, after the shoot.

"Then I'll be one of those people who only becomes famous after they're dead," she said, grinning.

"You'll be famous," I said.

"Promise?" she said, imitating a pout like a spoiled model.

"I promise."

Well Vicki, because of this book, I might be able to keep my promise to you. I hope those who read your story will share it with others so that you can become more famous than you ever thought possible.

34. The Volcano

Touring with the USO and speaking to kids on US military bases around the world has been a truly incredible journey. From Guantanamo Bay to Guam, Italy to England, Germany to Japan, I have performed in front of thousands of military kids.

While on one such a tour in Italy, I had the opportunity of meeting an eleven-year-old boy who was clearly in distress. His mother asked me to chat with him because he was having a tough time due to his father being deployed in Afghanistan. Alex was agitated, wringing his hands and squirming in his seat, and he would not look me in the eye.

"Dude," I said, "you look like you're unhappy." He nodded. "I think I have something that might help," I said. He glanced at me without lifting his head. "I know some of the dumbest jokes in the world," I said. He lifted his head and shrugged his shoulders.

I proceeded to tell him what I call my "DUH" jokes. Like the sign I saw on a treadmill at the gym which said, "If you pass out, stop exercising immediately." *Duh! If you pass out you'll be unconscious. You will NOT be exercising.* Or a sign I saw on a baby stroller that said, "Remove infant before storage." He burst out laughing after the first joke. As one would imagine, the jokes cleared the air between us and helped him to relax.

Between the jokes, I began to chat with him about how he was feeling about his father. After a while he began to pour his heart out. And goodness, did it pour. Tears rolled down his cheeks and his chest heaved as he told me that his father had been gone for fifteen months, came back for a number of months, and was gone again. He told me that he had sent his father some e-mails but his father had not responded.

To help comfort Alex, I reached into my bag and took out Coco, a little stuffed mouse we created to help console children in distress. I told him that Coco was a good listener and liked to help kids just like him. He clutched Coco to his chest for the rest of the time we talked. The more he was able to share his pain the better he seemed to feel.

I asked him what really makes him happy. "Watching TV," he said. Alex told me that he loved nature shows and liked stories about the sea and especially about volcanoes. Then he told me he had no friends and how much he hated moving from base to base. When I asked him why he had no friends, he told me he was scared to make friends because every time someone spoke to him he would shake inside.

"I know exactly what to do about that," I said.

"What?" he said, looking at me hopefully. I asked him to describe exactly what happens when he tries to make friends.

He said that when he meets new people he feels like he is shivering inside and he can't say what he is thinking.

I asked him to imagine that he was meeting some new people and to try and experience how it might feel if it were actually happening at that moment. He tensed up and started to look very anxious. "Tell me what you are feeling?" I asked.

"Like I want to explode inside," he said.

"Okay. I want you to close your eyes and think about what you are feeling inside." He closed his eyes. "All that anger and pain and frustration inside you is like a boiling volcano, right?" He nodded vigorously. "Right. I want you to feel all of that boiling sadness, anger and frustration bubbling in your feet like the volcanoes you see on TV. I want you to bring it up through your body and let it burst right out of the top of your head. Go for it." He clenched his teeth and squeezed, paused, then opened his eyes. "What happened?" I asked.

"It got stuck at the top of my head," he said, disappointed. I gently encouraged him to try again. He clenched his teeth and squeezed his whole body again. Then he suddenly opened his eyes and yelped with excitement. "It's out! I let it out!"

I could see the change in the boy immediately. He unclenched his fists, relaxed and was now sitting up straight and holding his head high. "How do you feel after that?" I asked.

"Confident," he said.

We both yelled excitedly and exchanged a high five. "The next time you have that feeling inside, do this exercise," I said. "It really works."

Alex was thrilled and walked out of the room smiling and

happy. His mother, who was talking to my business partner Woody at the time, burst into tears at her son's transformation. A camp counselor who was sitting quietly in the corner of the room while I was talking to Alex came out of the door behind us, crying openly.

"I have never seen anything like it," he said. "I wish I could do that."

"You can," I said, after Alex and his mother had gone. The counselor and I talked about what had happened with Alex. I told him that I believe it's all about listening to what children are asking for instead of telling them what we think they need to hear.

Alex called me later to say that he was so happy to meet me and that Coco missed me. His mother got in touch with me later to thank us and the USO for changing her child's life. That little boy, and all of the other children mentioned in this book, are why there is a Trevor Romain Foundation dedicated to making the world a better place for kids.

FOUNDATION

Building a Solid Foundation

I have spent many years visiting schools in support of my self-help books. The visits are in the form of a stand-up comedy routine where I tell the kids jokes and weave important information and anecdotes through my funny stories.

Although my talks are humor-based, I touch on a number of issues that children face, such as grief, divorce, bullying, and cancer. After almost every talk, children feel comfortable enough to come up and tell me their stories. Sometimes, they just spill their hearts out. What is truly incredible is to see the relief in their faces once they let go of their pain.

That relief, that letting go of pain, spurred many discussions with my business partners about how to develop our work with children—how to use our art, stories, and genuine compassion to help them. During one such discussion, we decided to create a Grief Comfort Kit for kids based on my book and video called *What On Earth Do You Do When Someone Dies?* Right away, there was a lot of interest in the kit from nonprofit organizations like the Candlelighters Childhood Cancer Foundation and Hospice.

Around this time, I took a trip to an orphanage in South Africa. I tried some of the exercises from the Grief Comfort Kit and was amazed by the results. It was after this trip that my partners, Woody and Ronda Englander, and I decided to promote this art of caring, and form a nonprofit foundation to help kids facing adversity.

We started by expanding our Grief Comforts Kits, adding a journal, book, video, colored pencils, and a personal note. The box that contains the kit also doubles as a memory box in which the grieving child can keep pictures, notes, and memories of the person who has died. Also included in the box is a wonderful stuffed mouse named Coco. He was aptly named by Ronda because he is like a cup of hot cocoa on a cold day: warm, inviting, and comforting. Coco has large ears so that he can listen to people's problems. Coco started as a doodle in my journal and has become our mascot and a true symbol of hope.

Starting as a doodle and turning into a dream, our comfort kits have been true to their name. We are so proud that these unique kits are now being used by the United States Department of Defense to comfort families of fallen troops fighting in Iraq, Afghanistan, and other conflict areas around the world. The kits have been adopted by the USO and are made available through them at Dover Air Force Base, where the bodies of fallen US troops are met by their grieving families.

Although many foundations seek to offer support to children, we have something unique. I have spoken to tens of thousands of school children around the world and have 20 years of experience working with children living with the effects of childhood cancer. In partnership with the United Nations and UNICEF, I have traveled to the Democratic Republic of Congo where I visited with children rehabilitating from their life as child soldiers. Additionally, I have completed several USO tours visiting schools on military bases in Guam, England, Germany, Japan, and Cuba delivering stand-up comedy and life lessons for kids. Our foundation was born out of our love for children and the work we have done to comfort kids across the world who are experiencing difficult circumstances. The combination of the professional resources of the Trevor Romain Company and my ability to connect with children—to make them laugh and give them hope—sets us apart.

The Trevor Romain Foundation is creating a series of comfort kits that are customized to meet children's specific needs. Whether a child has lost a family member, has a family member deployed in the military, has been diagnosed with cancer, or is living in war-torn areas of Africa, a comfort kit will be designed to include resources that are both educational and comforting to that child. These kits are an integral part of the Trevor Romain Foundation's goal to provide support and comfort to kids facing adversity.

For more information or to donate to
the Trevor Romain Foundation
please visit us at
TrevorRomainFoundation.org
or email us at info@TrevorRomainFoundation.org

Trevor Romain Foundation • 4412 Spicewood Springs • Suite 705 • Austin, TX 78759
phone 512.372.8359 • fax 512.480.8815

Acknowledgments

First, thanks to my *china plate,* Amiel, for continued love and support, and for putting up with me telling these stories 1,300,012 times.

Thanks to my family and other animals who appear in some of the adventures that take place in this book.

Thanks to Ronda Englander, who saw the light in a bunch of stories and helped guide, nurture, and turn those stories into the Trevor Romain Foundation, which she now heads.

To Woody and the Englander family, for their unwavering support.

To Steve Abrams, who took a bunch of my blogs, notes, sketches and ramblings and turned them into the book that you hold in your hands. Without Steve, this book would never have happened.

Thanks to Cory Rivademar, for the design, layout and for happily singing '70s songs during the making of this book.

To Coleen O'Hanley, for dropping everything to do meticulous copyediting and proofreading.

To the board of the Trevor Romain Foundation: Marita Frackowiak, Becky Hopkins, Jennifer Horne, Sharmila Kassam and Kierstan Schwab, thank you for your leadership.

Trevor Romain is a best-selling children's book author, award-winning video personality, and motivational speaker. He has traveled all over the world delivering his message of hope and compassion to school-age children. Trevor uses humor to engage the children, and then weaves in his messages to inspire kids to become better people and better friends to their peers. As the *Washington Post* said, "His rapport with kids is a stunning thing to watch." Trevor teaches kids how to manage some of the struggles that they face on a daily basis.

Trevor is well known for his work in the local and national community as a board member of the Candlelighters Childhood Cancer Foundation and Any Baby Can. The Trevor Romain Foundation was born out of his love for children and the work he has done to comfort kids across the world experiencing difficult circumstances.